D1103828

Security procedures for computer systems

Security procedures for computer systems

CHARLES F. HEMPHILL, JR.

M.S., Doctor of Jurisprudence
Senior Consultant
Loss Prevention Division
The Wackenhut Corporation

JOHN M. HEMPHILL

M.S., Ph.D.
Former Visiting Assistant Professor
of Computer Science and Electrical Engineering
Southern Methodist University, Consultant

1973
DOW JONES-IRWIN, INC.
Homewood, Illinois 60430

© DOW JONES-IRWIN, INC., 1973

This publication is designed to provide accurate and authoritative information in regard to the subject matter covered. It is sold with the understanding that the publisher is not engaged in rendering legal, accounting, or other professional service. If legal advice or other expert assistance is required, the services of a competent professional person should be sought.

> *From a Declaration of Principles jointly adopted by a Committee of the American Bar Association and a Committee of Publishers.*

First Printing, July 1973

ISBN 0-87094-058-9
Library of Congress Catalog Card No. 73-80100

Printed in the United States of America

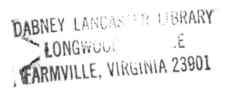

To
Phyllis,
Tom and Julie,
Bob and Linda,
Anita, and
Gregg

To
Susan

PREFACE

This book was written to provide guidelines for protection of the company or institutional computer.

Unless protective responsibilities for the computer are met, actual cases indicate that enormous business losses may be the eventual result.

A computer security program is typical of most other major functional areas of business. General management provides direction, establishing goals and setting policies. Systems specialists provide design, building security capabilities into the system. Operations management furnishes implementation, establishing and enforcing controls under which security operates. Meanwhile, the security department provides physical safeguards and procedures which protect the physical installation and personnel. It is through all these combined efforts that an effective program is maintained.

This book is intended to give management an outline of all security responsibilities. In addition, it was written to provide systems specialists, operations management, and members of the security department an understanding of the interlocking responsibilities of each other.

This is not a technical work. While many business employees may not understand some or all of the operations of the computer, it does not necessarily follow that they can ignore the need to safeguard the system. Neither management nor employees should remain unaware of the methods by which security is implemented.

To provide realistic protection, management must first examine the risks to which the individual computer and its support systems may be subjected. Then, responsible employees must plan and cooperate to eliminate or minimize each hazard.

If the procedures utilized are overly complicated, they will soon be discarded. Employee enthusiasm cannot be maintained under such circumstances.

And while employee support will waiver, the need for security will continue.

The information in this book is not intended as a prescription for a loss-free installation. It can only be a guide in designing and maintaining a system for computer security.

The authors owe a considerable debt for the constructive help and encouragement offered by Professor Gwyn Belles of Rio Hondo College, Whittier, California; Dr. Cliff Hemming, Jr., of the University of Texas Southwestern Medical School, Dallas, Texas; Dr. Richard Thomas of Bowling Green State University, Bowling Green, Ohio; and B. E. Gorrill of the Wackenhut Corporation, Coral Gables, Florida. Susan Hemphill and Anita Hemphill assisted in manuscript preparation. Ross Hemphill furnished legal advice; Clarence Sutphin advised concerning insurance.

June 1973   Charles F. Hemphill, Jr.
                     John M. Hemphill

CONTENTS

right registration. Patentability. New legislation.
Code of ethics.

17
Insurance to protect the computer

Some unusual losses. Insurance coverage. Equipment insurance. Media insurance. Errors and omissions insurance. Business interruption insurance. Extra-expense insurance. Loss of accounts receivable. Special indemnity bonds. Directors and officers liability insurance. Reducing insurance premiums. Insurance claims.

INTRODUCTION

1

In all ages man has dreamed of using machines to lighten his load. With the coming of the "information explosion," Electronic Data Processing (EDP) greatly increased man's ability to store, retrieve, manipulate, and transmit vital information. And after the initial novelty wore off, the computer became almost commonplace. Today, it is the very nerve center of commercial life.

Yet there is no single factor in trade or industry that surpasses the computer in its potential to cripple or destroy an entire business quickly.

Ignoring the risks involved, some firms continue to utilize the advantages of the computer but claim that they cannot afford an effective loss prevention program. But "security is a judgmental game played against unknown adversaries plotting unknown harm at unknown times and places."[1] The costs of computer protection must be balanced against the tremendous risks involved.

An institution or business that cannot afford adequate computer security cannot afford a computer operation.

Dependence on the computer

Almost any business which has introduced an Electronic Data Processing system into its basic operations will agree with the observation that increased use of the computer will almost invariably lead to greater dependency on that computer.

Also, there is a growing reliance by present-day management on computer information, not only for financial data, but also in such interests as production, forecasting, marketing, engineering, and development.

Inadequate security

Notwithstanding this increased reliance on the computer, companies that in the past prided themselves on alert, conscientious management may yet

---

[1] Walter A. Kleinschrod, "A Game of Cost and Risk," reprinted from *Administrative Management*, © 1971 by Geyer-McAllister Publications, Inc.

lack a computer security program, or may have inadequate protection at best.

Natural or man-made disasters may cause some damage, regardless of the precautions that management may take, but actual cases indicate that management often deliberately chooses to ignore the possibilities for serious harm.

A security program may never be foolproof, but management can work toward this goal. It is one thing to introduce a new security program at a computer installation, and quite another to implement the system until it provides good protection.

Reasons for lack of security

Due to habit, some computer professionals continue to tolerate a high level of risk. In commenting on this lack of security, a number of qualified observers have pointed out that some businesses rely on nothing more than the ignorance of outside individuals to be their principal defense against loss of computerized data.

Undoubtedly, some of this inadequacy in the security field stems from the manner in which businesses and institutions plunged into the computer era. "Twinkling lights, spinning tapes, and pastel cabinets seem to have a mesmerizing effect on some managers. [They were] in a pell-mell rush to be the first to play with a new toy. . . ."[2] As pointed out by one authority:

The reasons seem to be partly historical and partly psychological.

The history of EDP in most companies has been one of continuous crash projects. The imposition of rigid controls and security systems would indeed have been ludicrous, when getting a program to run at all was a major accomplishment. Although some EDP centers still run on a crash basis, most of them have settled down sufficiently so that internal controls can and ought to be implemented.[3]

[2] A. R. Zipf, "Retaining Mastery of the Computer," *Harvard Business Review*, September–October 1968, p. 70.

[3] Brandt Allen, "Danger Ahead! Safeguard Your Computer," *Harvard Business Review*, November–December 1968, p. 99.

One of the factors which may have delayed the installation of security controls is the very complexity of EDP systems. Unless company officials have been actively involved in learning something of the operation of the computer, there may be a tendency to attribute a mystical, infallible quality to it. This attitude assumes that the very complexity of the operation makes the computer immune to misuse or deliberate fraud.

Thinking of this kind ignores the purpose for which the machine was built—to do whatever the operator directs. And sometimes the real vulnerability may be in "doctoring" of data before input. No computer can tell the difference between valid and inaccurate, or even dishonest, information.

As previously pointed out, another factor which often figures in lack of computer security is that of cost. Those who realize the dangers are frequently not the same businessmen who hold the purse strings. Then too, senior executives who have overall responsibility for computer security may feel that they have more immediate business problems. But management, production, and sales employees must all become, in fact, computer people. A good computer security program generates confidence in any business. In many instances it may even be a saleable feature of the business itself.

But total security is an ideal. The closer to this objective, the greater the cost. The question is sometimes asked whether a computer can ever be completely protected against all conceivable hazards. As more complexities are added to the protection of the computer and its operations, then more time and money are needed by the people who use it. Consequently, at some point there may be a compromise between costs and objectives.

The potentials for damage to a computer system **Potential dangers**
are many, including economic, operational, and legal problems. Damage may be the outgrowth of a malicious act, a natural disaster, or nothing more sinister than operational carelessness.

Any fire, flood, earthquake, or structural failure of the building may destroy the system. Procedural errors can erase vital information. Mechanical problems, attributable to faulty equipment may be almost as destructive.

Sabotage of files or computer hardware by a disgruntled or deranged employee is another feared risk, as is deliberate destruction of an entire computer installation by a militant group.

The possible loss of essential data while converting records from a manual operation to a computer system is another definite threat. Then too, employee embezzlement of assets represents a continuing danger in the operation of a computer accounting system, just as it does in a manual accounting system.

Legal responsibility of company directors

It is a broad principle of American law that every director of a corporation is legally obligated to use the same degree of care in the performance of his corporate duties that a reasonable, prudent man would use in his own private business. What, then, is the responsibility of a corporate director who fails to provide proper security for a computer?

The answer, of course, will vary from case to case. But as a general propositon, the corporate director is legally obligated to repay his firm for all losses resulting from his failure to exercise due care. It is of little concern here as to how a lawsuit of this kind would be initiated. Eventually, the matter would be settled through a jury determination as to whether a reasonable, prudent man would have insisted on better computer controls and verification procedures than were actually used by the corporation. Since the jury would receive this matter for consideration only after loss had become an established fact, it is quite likely that the jury would reach a verdict against a director who had in any manner neglected computer security.

Then too, under Section 11 of the Securities Act of 1933, officers of a corporation who sign securities registration statements are legally liable to stockholders for any misleading omission of fact. In case of computer fraud, Section 11 of this act would apply to failure of the corporate officer to completely describe computer accounting controls in the securities registration statement.

A desire to avoid personal liability then, if nothing more, should induce all corporate and institutional officers to provide for the installation of basic security controls in all computer installations.

Although it could be desirable to avoid the expense and effort of installing security controls, the risks to both directors and the corporation are too great.

Management has long recognized that stringent controls are necessary in manual bookkeeping and accounting systems, if employee fraud is to be avoided. It is apparent that computer systems are also vulnerable. In fact, under many circumstances, the computer risks may be greater. "An erasure is usually detectable in a ledger book, but there is no practical way to find out by inspection what used to be recorded on a magnetic tape or even if it has been changed."[4]

It is also worth noting that the records of practically all businesses contain some proprietary secrets. The competitive position of almost any company will suffer if its trade secrets become public knowledge. It is indicated, then, that a program to protect machines, records, and software must be utilized.

One slowly developing trend during recent years seems to be the designation of a responsible, top level official in larger companies, with primary responsibility to direct the corporate computer program. This may be a basic step in establishing an effective security program.

Centralization of responsibility

[4] Robert V. Jacobson, "Providing Security Protection for Computer Files," *Best's Review*, May 1970, p. 42.

On the other hand, high level management in some firms is still unaware of the level of data processing risks, and delegates authority for important decisions in this area too far down the line.

It is suggested that at least one senior executive should be able to give informed answers to questions about existing hazards. But no one official or class of employees should be expected to bear complete responsibility for security. The need for controls should be brought home to all personnel in the organization, beginning with top management and extending to all employees. It is helpful for a protection philosophy to permeate the whole company or organization. And this philosophy should, of course, operate within a self-imposed framework of practicality.

Regardless of the number of employees in the Electronic Data Processing installation, it may be preferable for one official to have overall responsibility.

Follow-up

Once established, the requirements of the security protection plan should be regularly reviewed and procedures verified. This program is necessary because security requirements change from time to time. Unless there is continuing verification, employees overlook compliance. If proper attitudes are not maintained, vital procedures may very well be ignored.

Detached specialists

In some companies it may be found that an Electronic Data Processing security system cannot be sustained without the services of one or more technically skilled computer security specialists, who function independently of computer line management. These specialists should audit and verify any or all control procedures at unannounced times.

It is the responsibility of these detached specialists to immediately inform EDP line management of any breach of approved procedures.

Scope of protection

Perhaps no two computer installations will have the same requirements for security. But some broad, general principles may be followed in almost every instance.

Properly conceived, the loss prevention program should extend to all computer hardware and software areas—hardware being the physical equipment of the computer system, and software the programs and routines it uses.

To be effective, protection must combine control of physical access to the installation, as well as other aspects. Physical security measures, alone, are not enough; neither are processing restrictions that only serve to regulate software access. A personnel security program should also be included, to develop and retain the kind of technicians and employees that make security measures work.

Computer security is the sum of many parts. A meaningful program will usually represent a blend of those interlocking components—an interface of physical protection, procedural safeguards, and personnel selection, backed up by audit controls and insurance to compensate in case of loss. All this necessitates cooperation between data processing areas and the financial and security departments.

Where possible, each of the individual controls should be built into the system at the outset, rather than added on at a later time. It should also be emphasized that an effective program is a continuing one, following through all operations, even to the destruction of tape and/or other data.

It may be a mistake to assume that one aspect of a security plan is of more value for protection than any other. There should be an integration of all the interdependent features, as pictured in Illustration 1 on page 8.

It is the purpose of the chapters that follow to acquaint business and data processing employees with the vulnerabilities of the computer, and to present a loss prevention system framework upon which an organization may develop and build to satisfy individual needs.

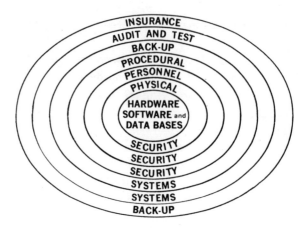

Illustration 1.
Integrated requirements
of a computer security
plan

Check off list

1.

Has management planned protection, not only for computer hardware, but for software access and record storage as well?

2.

Do corporate or industrial directors realize that they may be personally liable for neglecting computer security, or for failure to set up adequate auditing procedures to detect computer fraud?

3.

Does one responsible official have overall charge of computer activity?

4.

Has provision been made to follow up basic security planning?

5.

Is it understood by systems specialists, operating personnel, and security representatives that there is an interlocking dependency and responsibility for computer security?

AVOIDING NATURAL AND
PHYSICAL DISASTERS

2

Essentially, there are two kinds of catastrophes. One is man-made, and the other appears as the wrath of nature. But regardless of the origin, either kind of disturbance may cause serious economic losses to Electronic Data Processing installations.

Some of the man-made upheavals may involve damage by riots and industrial sabotage. The natural physical disasters most commonly encountered include accidental fire, flooding, structural failure (building collapse), explosion, tornado, hurricane, or earthquake.

Of these natural catastrophes, fire is probably the most serious security threat; and as an aftermath of some other calamities, such as explosion or earthquake, fire may be a secondary cause of damage, increasing the amount of loss. The hazards that are involved in computer fires are discussed in a separate chapter in this book.

Recounting some of the misfortunes that have struck computer sites may appear to be a mere listing of incidents in a recitation of disaster. But an analysis of details in some of these cases will focus attention on the risks that management should seek to avoid or to minimize by advance planning. Often, proper site selection can do much to eliminate the likelihood of serious loss.

From a security viewpoint, the best location for a **General security** computer room is one of isolation. In general, it is preferable to house the entire computer operation in a separate building. An upper floor, interior location is frequently recommended, although a secure ground floor may be just as desirable. At any rate, it should be an area that does not readily permit unauthorized access. Quite frequently, however, the computer must be located in an existing building, and this almost always poses more troublesome security problems than a new building.

Ideally, the installation should be located out of

the main traffic flow, behind substantial walls, and away from public reception areas.

If security is to be effective, planning should be directed toward two objectives:

1. Obtaining a site that restricts unauthorized individuals or groups who may be responsible for man-made disasters, and
2. Selecting a site that will eliminate many of the possibilities of environmental and natural hazards.

An additional consideration in selecting a computer site is accessibility to police and fire fighting facilities.

Civil disturbances

An ideal location must, of course, satisfy operational requirements. Public transportation, including safe access to bus or transportation lines, is a basic necessity.

From a civic and geographic standpoint, it is desirable that the neighborhood be attractive to the technicians and computer professionals needed to staff the operation. Due to the high cost of equipment, many computer centers operate on a three-shift, twenty-four-hour day. Some employees must necessarily arrive and depart during the hours of darkness. If the neighborhood has a high rate of serious crime, it may be difficult to persuade employees to work there, even if the building and parking areas are well lighted and protected at all times. Female employees, especially those working the second and third shifts, are hesitant to drive through such a neighborhood in getting to work.

The police department in most metropolitan areas can furnish figures regarding crime rates and local criminal activities in a specific area. If the number of "purse snatchings," robberies, thefts, and attempted assaults is below average, these facts should be considered as favorable in site selection. Then too, police response and the frequency of police patrols are other factors to be examined.

The site chosen for a computer center should be

an area that can be expected to remain free from riots and civil disturbances. There are no hard and fast rules that can be counted on to provide immunity from future problems. But some locations obviously have more potential for danger in regard to this type of calamity. Definite inquiries into the history of mass demonstrations, riots, and civil disturbances throughout the area should be considered.

Management cannot be expected to foresee all of the possible risks of fire, flood, earthquake, hurricane, or structural failure of the building. But there should be definite planning to avoid most of these risks long before they may materialize.

Natural forces

Some of the most violent upheavals in nature give little notice of their coming force. Others, however, can be anticipated, at least a short period in advance. While there may be no way to halt destructive forces already unleashed, it is often possible to take advantage of the warning period to improve protective measures and to minimize loss.

On the other hand, there may be no prior warning in the event of an explosion or an earthquake. Planning at the time the site is chosen would appear to be the answer here.

Most of the potential for flood damage centers around locations where rivers or waterways overflow, or where there is inadequate building drainage. Some actual cases in this regard are enlightening.

Flooding

A Texas company recently advised a security consultant that the firm planned to install a computer complex in a comparatively low-lying area near the Trinity River in the Fort Worth, Texas, area. The property had been selected as a desirable computer site since it was conveniently near company headquarters, retail outlets, and major freeway connections. But officials who had selected this site did not bother to find out that floods had seriously damaged many nearby businesses on three separate occasions in the prior thirty years. High waters in the future would almost certainly cause damage.

But all water damage may not result from locating

the computer center where it may be subjected to overflowing lakes or rivers. Damage may result from bursting water pipes or from plugged storm drains that cause water to back up. Recently, a small computer installation at Dallas, Texas, was damaged seriously under tons of water and roofing materials. The computer was housed on a first floor level, with areas from the second floor draining on to the flat roof above the computer room. The drainage system was constructed so that all runoff above the computer room would drain into a storm sewer. When the roof drains above the first floor became plugged with trash, the weight of the accumulated water broke down the roof structure. The downpour of water and roofing materials caused considerable damage to both computer hardware and software. An engineer stated that an adequate drainage system, properly maintained, would have avoided the loss.

In a recent security survey of a New Jersey company, it was observed that the firm's computer was located in the basement of the building. The company maintained that the following benefits could be attributed to this basement location:

1. Ease in controlling security access;
2. Nearness to air conditioning and auxiliary power units;
3. Ease in controlling humidity and temperature in operating areas; and
4. Reduced construction costs.

All of these enumerated benefits may be very desirable. But, here again, the advantages of the basement location would be quickly cancelled out if a broken water main on an upper floor could not be immediately drained off.

In some individual installations, outside water may be controlled by installing curbs and lips on all doors leading into computer rooms. These devices are not adequate to keep out water under actual flood conditions, however.

In another case, a consultant found the computer room in a Philadelphia bank was eight feet below grade. Examination of the building revealed that there were no floor drains. Activation of the building's fire sprinkler system could quickly pour large quantities of water into the basement location. This room had previously been used by the building engineer, and there was a sizeable sump pit underneath the floor. It was recommended that an adequately engineered drainage system be installed, so that water could not accumulate in the computer room. This recommendation was rejected by the bank, however, because of the cost. It was then recommended as an alternative that a pump be installed in the sump pit, and this proposal was put into effect. The pump was automatically activated if water should begin to rise in the pit. An alarm system was also installed, alerting the engineer and a central alarm station of the possibility for flooding.

This case seems to illustrate some of the hazards that may be anticipated when a computer system must be located in an existing building. If there is a possibility for serious water damage from a floor above, it is suggested that remodeling plans include a poured concrete roof over the computer room, or at least a waterproof membrane in the ceiling.

Remodeling plans for a computer center in Florida specified a second floor location. All walls, floors, and ceilings of this structure were of poured concrete. A study of the drawings of this large building revealed that a four-inch water main was located between an outer concrete and an inner sheetrock partition of the room selected to house the computer library.

While earthquakes are not likely in Florida, any accidental rupture of this water main would probably flood the tape library. Damage resulting from an accident of this kind could be quite serious, as the solid concrete floors and walls could be expected to hold the flooding waters inside the computer center.

Desirable recommendations to prevent this possibility of damage could involve rerouting the water main, or relocating the tape library in another area of the building; but either of these changes would be very expensive.

In the building being remodeled, there had once been an outlet for drainage in the basic concrete floor, 18 inches beneath the raised computer floor. This drainage outlet had been sealed during the preliminary stages of remodeling, to prevent the possible spread of fire from a lower floor.

Construction engineers advised that installation of either a "flap valve" or "check valve" in the cement floor would allow the drainage of large amounts of water into the area below. When consulted, local fire department officials pointed out that installation of either of these valves would be acceptable under existing fire codes. Accordingly, a "flap valve" was installed.

Explosions

On August 23, 1966, a blast caused by escaping natural gas completely destroyed a Honeywell H-200 leased computer system and related equipment at the Phelps Dodge Copper Company, Fort Wayne, Indiana. The installation was valued in excess of $290,000.

As one witness put it, "The computer, with a 16K core memory and four tape drives, was for all practical purposes destroyed." IBM gear lost in the blast consisted of a 407, a sorter, and a "roomful of keypunch and verifier equipment."

It may be argued with some logic that a disaster of this kind could never be anticipated or avoided. On the other hand, it may reflect good planning to locate any computer installation at some distance from a gas-fueled boiler room. Also, if potentially explosive chemicals or products are manufactured or used in the area, it may be desirable to locate the computer operation in an isolated building.

There is frequently an unusual potential for explosion or fire in an area around a business safe. This is because professional burglars sometimes utilize nitroglycerin or dynamite to blow open the

Illustration 2.
Wreckage of the Phelps
Dodge Copper Company
building, Fort Wayne,
Indiana, August 23, 1966,
caused by natural gas
explosion

safe, or cut into it with an acetylene-burning torch. Since these burglary techniques increase the possibilities of computer damage by explosion or fire, it is recommended that the computer be located at some distance from a company money safe. Since the acetylene torch is an unusual fire hazard under any circumstances, it is considered dangerous to allow welding in the vicinity of the computer.

Earthquakes

Most recent earthquake activity has been centered in the western states, principally in California. This has not always been the case, and there is no certainty that this will continue in the future.

The gigantic earthquake that centered around New Madrid, Missouri, in December 1811, may have been far more powerful than any other calamity of this kind that has been reported in the Western Hemisphere. Damage around the center of this quake was apparently slight, because the area was thinly populated. This phenomenon was of such

15

proportions, however, that it was felt in Boston, half a continent away.

Today, maps are available showing the specific locations of geological faults that have been active in the recent past. Millions of dollars have been spent by the federal government on research, and quite a lot is known about geologically young or active faults. If the company has a choice, it may be preferable to select a computer location that is not near an active fault. Good building construction will also help.

A major distributing company in the Hollywood, California area suffered considerable damage in the computer library during the earthquake of February 9, 1971. Some of the ceiling collapsed here, while large cabinets toppled over, spilling tangled computer tapes onto the floor about the time the ceiling fell.

Engineers stated that the damage here would have been slight had the tape racks been secured to the wall or securely fastened to the floor. With the benefit of hindsight, computer managers in earthquake-prone areas may insist that tape cabinets and computer hardware be adequately attached to the walls or floor of the building. In most locations this precaution would not be justified.

Hurricanes or storms   Hurricanes, tornadoes, and cyclones have all taken their toll in damage at computer installations. For example, the hurricane "Carla" completely destroyed a Burrough's computer in the plant of a major chemical company at Freeport, Texas, in 1963. News accounts following hurricane "Celia" in 1970 pointed out that several computers had been damaged at Corpus Christi, Texas. Windstorms in inland areas, including tornadoes and cyclones, have also caused their share of loss.

If the original building construction is such as to minimize possible damage from windstorm or high water, management's expenditures and planning may be completely justified.

Hazards from aircraft   A merchandising firm recently installed a computer complex at the end of a busy airport runway. Other sites in the neighborhood were available at comparable costs, but the location chosen was selected for easy access to the airport. A plane crash in the area may never affect the operation of this EDP center, but the potential for a physical disaster appears to have been increased by the placement of this building. On the other hand, a major airlines may feel compelled to utilize a location near an airport, so that administrative operations can be centralized.

Some computer centers utilize a helicopter to bring materials from outlying areas for processing. A major bank in a southeastern state located the landing space for their helicopter on the reinforced concrete roof of the computer building. Since the roof was of completely fireproof material, the officers of this bank saw no harm in locating the heliport immediately over the tape library and operating room. The potential danger here, however, was that the gas tank on the helicopter could be ruptured by an unusually rough landing, spraying as much as 200 gallons of flaming gasoline along the walls and windows of the building. Then too, there was always the possibility that the burning fuel mixture could run down into the building through the rooftop doorway.

In November 1969, a small plane landed on the roof of a building in Princeton, New Jersey, when the pilot ran out of gas. The plane caught fire, and two levels of the three-story building were destroyed by the flames. A computer in this building and some card files and tapes were lost. Most of the computer tapes and hardware were located on the ground floor and were saved when firemen were able to play hoses on the computer and these tapes.

The computer center for a midwestern municipal government was housed in an old masonry building that had long been in need of modernization. The EDP center operated on a two-shift basis, five days a week. Returning to work on a Monday morning,

Environmental damage

the computer supervisor found that the building had been sandblasted by an outside contractor on the previous Saturday. Although some of the city officials had long known that the sandblasting was to take place, they did not have the foresight to inform the computer center. A very fine, almost invisible dust had sifted all through the building as a result of the blasting process, with these particles settling in the computer hardware and disc packs. As a result, some of the discs could not be copied.

In all probability, covering computer components and discs in advance would have prevented the damage. Because of instances of this kind, it may be desirable for management to be reminded that any change in the environment around the computer should be brought to the attention of the computer supervisor.

In another case of industrial damage, a commercial firm was forced to spend $76,000 to reconstruct data stored on magnetic tapes when acid fumes partially destroyed the company's tape library. When the computer was originally located in this neighborhood, it was known that sulphuric acid fumes were released into the atmosphere as a waste product by a nearby manufacturing plant. The full potential for damage was not realized until loss actually occurred. Recovery of damages in a lawsuit against the polluting manufacturer would be legally possible. As a practical matter, however, it could be difficult to prove that the acid alone caused the damage. There would also be a question as to whether court awarded damages would completely cover the loss of business momentum that had resulted.

There must also be protection of the immediate surroundings. Expensive computer hardware and software at one location was lost in a fire because it was on a second floor, directly above a highly flammable paint shop.

In another recent case, a firm that maintained a computer went to considerable effort to upgrade fire protection in the immediate location. Comparable protection was not provided on other floors of the building, apparently because of the expense. When fire broke out on the first floor, there was no direct damage on the second floor, in the area of the computer. The intensity of the blaze, however, caused the first floor ceiling to collapse, dropping the entire computer center into the flames.

Radar and microwave emissions can interfere with the operation of the computer central processing unit itself, causing errors. In effect, the computer acts as an antenna for the radio waves. Radar at an airport may be one of the troublesome sources of electromagnetic radiation in cases of this kind. But other sources of electromagnetic radiation, such as nearby arc welding, can cause interference. Usually these sources of radiation present no problem unless they are very close and powerful sources. In choosing a satisfactory location for a system, however, management should not overlook this potential threat.

Electromagnetic damage

Several years ago the processing center of the U.S. Internal Revenue Service at Austin, Texas, reportedly lost information on several reels of tape that contained income tax returns. Data on the tapes was erased by energy emitted from the radar at a nearby airport.

Computerworld magazine reported in December 1970, that thousands of tax records on tapes belonging to the U.S. Internal Revenue office at Nashville, Tennessee, had been erased by airport radar. It is to be noted that these tapes were maintained about 200 yards from the radar installation.

Check off list

1.
Is the site chosen one that seems free from the possibility of riots or civil disorders? A crime-free area?

2.
Is the neighborhood such that female employees will be willing to work during night hours (second and third shifts)?

19

3.
Does the site selected seem to minimize the risks of (a) fire, (b) flood, (c) windstorm, (d) explosion, (e) earthquake, and other physical disasters?

4.
Is the computer subject to possible flooding in a basement location, or because of a ruptured water main or storm drain?

5.
Is the computer area removed from the building paint shop (fire hazard), boiler room (explosive hazard), or company safe (danger from burglar's acetylene torch)?

6.
Does a gasoline-laden helicopter, bringing input data to the computer installation, present a possible fire danger?

7.
Is the computer located near explosive manufacturing proccesses, stairwells, open courts, or a receiving dock?

8.
Should there be shielding against radar and microwave interference?

PHYSICAL SECURITY

In many respects, physical protection for a computer installation follows closely the kind of security measures used by business to prevent theft, burglary, and other crimes against property. If there is a door, secure it; if there is an area that gives easy access, fence it; if there is a dark area, light it. Sometimes these protective requirements are so commonplace that it is assumed they are always adequate and operable. But frequently, effectiveness is never verified. Without good physical security, most other measures designed to protect the computer system become sharply devalued.

It is desirable to evelute the benefits that may be expected from each individual protective device or installation. Physical controls should be tailored to the needs of the individual site. To utilize either more or less physical security may be inadequate or wasteful.

In assessing the needs of the computer location, it is to be noted that there are now hundreds of protective alarms, devices, locks, and items of security hardware on the market. Many of these have wide application. Others may be of great value under some circumstances, but are of doubtful use in others. A professional security consultant can advise as to performance, dependability, and cost of various devices; but there are certain basic principles that will serve as security guidelines for any computer installation.

The physical site of a computer installation can itself be a means of providing protection.

Building site

In the first place, it is usually desirable to have a separate building, used solely for computer activities. Physical access is usually easier to set up and maintain in a single-purpose building. Then too, the requirements of security can be more easily enforced under such circumstances. Ideally, the computer building should be located a reasonable distance from other structures. This serves to make intruders more conspicuous and prevents the spread of fire from nearby structures.

On the other hand, it is sometimes possible to take advantage of security programs that are already in force in an existing building, and a separate building may be more vulnerable to deliberate attack. All in all, however, the separate building is to be preferred.

With regard to sensitive areas in a computer installation, the machine room, the tape and disc library, data preparation areas, forms storage areas, and air conditioning and electrical distribution systems should all be included.

In general, it is preferable to locate the machine room and the library well within the interior of the building. This is preferable to a location along exterior walls, since a bomb placed against an outside wall could still cause damage inside.

Masses of shrubbery and trees, planted near a building, often provide cover for intruders. While the esthetic value of these plantings is unquestioned, it is desirable to assure unobstructed visibility of approaches to the building.

Preferably, utilities should be underground. This prevents roof access to the building by climbing utility poles. Underground access also affords some concealment of utilities from a would-be saboteur. If the computer is housed in a row of buildings, roof access may be relatively easy from structures on either side. To protect against intrusion from the roof area, a chain link type fence may be located at any wall where access is possible from an adjoining building.

Lighting

In the darkness of night, a computer center may seem relatively silent and isolated, even though it is in operation 24 hours a day. With adequate lighting the building becomes a landmark in the night, unapproachable except openly. Among persons with security experience, there is general agreement that good lighting is one of the most effective deterrents to keep out the unwanted. Good interior lighting is also beneficial, resulting in better interior security, safety, and efficiency.

Engineering assistance is usually needed in planning lighting systems for effectiveness and economy. In general, security lighting outside the building does not require intense illumination. The needs will usually vary, however, with a minimum of 20-footcandle power being used at critical entrances and to illuminate outside work areas. A minimum of only 0.5-footcandle power may be needed in some other locations. In any event, employee entrances, exits, and parking lots should be adequately lighted, along with the perimeter of the building. As a rough test, if the subheads of an average newspaper can be easily read on the parking lot, then visibility is generally adequate for employee protection.

One of the problems with security lighting is that employees frequently forget to turn on the system, especially if there is no night shift on duty at the computer system. This can be solved by using an automatic timer, eliminating the possibility for human error.

All fixtures will burn out at times, and the light patterns should be such that failure of a single lamp does not leave an entire area in darkness. A regular inspection program by the building engineer will maintain replacements at an adequate level.

Fencing

Like night lighting, a fence will not in itself prevent unauthorized intrusion, but if properly installed and used, a fence will provide good control of approaches to the building.

Some business officials prefer a masonry wall or a wooden fence to one of chain link, since there is sometimes a feeling that the latter installation causes the property to resemble "a detention barracks or a penitentiary." It should be noted, however, that the construction of a solid wall or wooden fence does not permit observation from the outside into the interior of the property. And on the other hand, some types of open metal fencing are quite decorative.

To be effective, a chain link fence should be at least eight feet high, topped by three equally spaced strands of barbed wire. This wire is most effective when mounted on arms that extend both outward and inward at a 45-degree angle. The chain link should be drawn taut and securely fastened to heavy metal posts, firmly embedded in concrete. Posts should not be spaced more than ten feet apart, with adequate bracing at corners, terminals, and gates. It is recommended that the chain link wire be attached to the pavement or secured to the ground, to prevent "rolling up" the bottom of the fence or "tunneling."

Frequently, gates are the weakest areas in a fence line, and it is preferable that gates be locked with a post locking bar and a padlock.

The hardware fixtures that secure the chain link fabric are usually bolted. In many cases the nuts can be removed from the bolts in a matter of minutes by use of hand tools. When this happens, a section of fence may then be pulled from the post. But if the bolts are bradded with a hammer at the time of installation, it is usually very difficult to remove them.

Locks and keys

A well-designed lock-and-key system is a vital part of security in any computer building, with master keys issued on the basis of the center's organizational chart. Each organization should have access only to areas within its own jurisdiction; but for practicality, all janitor's closets or all doors involving a particular maintenance function throughout the building may be keyed alike.

While the building is under construction, temporary cylinders can be used for security, and replaced when the contractor has no further need for access.

If the building is a large one, it may be helpful to prepare drawings showing lock standards and key systems. It is also suggested that codes or numbers be stamped on locks and keys so that supervisors or others who must have access under emergency conditions will know which key to use.

It is essential that keys should be issued only on

the basis of need, and never as a status symbol. Unless good records of issuance are maintained, management is apt to lose control. If this should occur, it is recommended that locks be immediately changed.

Ideally, good physical security may best be maintained in a building constructed of reinforced, poured concrete, with walls, floors, and ceilings of the same material. As will be repeated throughout this book, this type of construction eliminates many of the computer problems associated with unauthorized entry and with the problems of computer fire.

Construction requirements

In theory, at least, entry and exit should be restricted to a single door, with no windows. This is because each door or window represents a potential opening for unauthorized entry. As a practical matter, however, a building with only one exit could be a serious firetrap. In most locations it is therefore necessary to include emergency fire doors that are openable from the inside, but that remain locked from the outside. If these are connected with an audible alarm, then an unauthorized exit will be immediately apparent to computer management.

Plans may include a freight door, to be opened only on those rare occasions when it is necessary to bring heavy equipment or computer hardware into the building. This freight door should, of course, remain locked at all other times, with keys rigidly controlled.

In an existing building, it may be desirable to seal all windows with brick or reinforced masonry. If exterior windows cannot be eliminated from the architectural plan, then they should be covered with a heavy grade of steel mesh, welded to the window frame or secured to the building wall.

An alternate solution might be to replace window glass with security glass or break-resistant plastic panels. However, these materials could not be expected to be as effective as heavy steel mesh.

It is also worth noting that decorative styles of mesh are available to conform to a number of different building schemes. From the standpoint of security, steel mesh is to be preferred to heavy steel window bars, since bars are separated enough to allow large objects such as a "Molotov cocktail" to be thrown through the window.

At an East Coast computer location, a large double window on the second floor was equipped with hinges and used as an entryway for computer freight. Ground floor doors and windows were adequately secured and protected at this location, but locking hardware was never installed on upper floor windows. An individual with average agility could swing up on to the canopy underneath this window and gain access to the second floor computer room which was just inside.

Apertures

Actual cases illustrate the potential hazards that may appear when there are unnecessary breaks in a building wall. For example, fire damage in the amount of $10,000 was caused in a U.S. government office at San Jose, California, during May 1972, when militants reportedly inserted an incendiary device into a mail slot.[1]

A somewhat similar incident recently occurred at Dallas, Texas. A garden hose used to water a small plot of grass was habitually left outside the building at this location. On a weekend, vandals inserted the hose into an unused mail slot in a door and turned on the water.

The room inside the door was the company computer room. While the exterior door had been permanently sealed, closing the unused mail slot had been overlooked. The water from the garden hose continued to run throughout the weekend, causing damage and requiring a "drying out period."

The student attack against the computer at Fresno State College (now a branch of the University of California) in May 1970 illustrates the vulnerability of unprotected windows. A CDC 3150 computer was destroyed by two "Molotov cocktails" thrown

---

[1] "Spectacular Marina Fire," *San Francisco Chronicle*, May 10, 1972, p. 18.

through windows by two students walking past. The computer was located only a few feet from these ground floor windows, "with nothing except window glass and venetian blinds between the processor and the street."

An attack of the type that occurred at Fresno caused some computer centers to brick up windows or to install steel mesh covers. A number of computer installations, however, continued to operate without window protection after the Fresno incident. *Datamation* reported in October 1970 that "at Queen's College of the City University of New York, the data processing personnel have been instructed to keep blinds down as 'protection' from firebombs."[2]

Doors and windows are not the only openings in the building shell that cause concern from the security standpoint. Trash chutes, dumbwaiter shafts, and coal chutes should also be protected.

The trash chute

In a loss prevention survey at a major East Coast business location it was found that a large metal trash chute extended downward from the second floor computer room to an unattended storage area on the first floor. This was a round, metal-lined chute, equipped with a lockable door on the upper floor. The lower end of the chute was fitted with a closable metal door, activated by a spring connected to a fusible metal link designed to melt in the event of fire. When utilized, this arrangement would close the lower chute door if fire broke out.

In evaluating the security problems at this location, it was found that the fusible metal link arrangement was no longer used. It was also found that trash and combustibles were allowed to accumulate in great quantities in the room underneath the computer. In addition, employees were careless in throwing cigarette butts on the floor in this area.

[2] F. Barry Nelson, "Campus Computers: Targets for Militants and Almost Anyone Else," reprinted with permission of *Datamation*®; copyright, Technical Publishing Co., Greenwich, CT, 06830, 1970.

Illustration 3.
Computer room damage
through unprotected
window, Fresno State
College (now University),
May 1970

It was obvious that the trash chute could serve as a "chimney" to carry fire from the lower floor into the computer room.

To control this fire danger, it was recommended that the door on the lower end of the trash chute be activated with the spring and fusible metal link. It was also recommended that the metal door at the top of the chute remain locked, except when trash was actually being dumped. In addition, it was suggested that large quantities of trash not be allowed to accumulate, and that a "no smoking" rule be enforced in that part of the building.

Of additional interest, the metal trash chute was wide enough that an intruder could easily climb up the chute by means of a short ladder available on the first floor. While officials at this computer center closely regulated second floor access to the computer room doors, there was no control over access to the first floor. Recommendations were made to control access to the first floor as well.

There was an additional security problem at this location, under the procedures being followed. The entry door to the tape library was no more than 20 feet from the upper end of the trash chute. An employee in the computer room, desiring to commit sabotage or to steal individual tapes, could throw tapes down the trash chute when no one was observing. These tapes could then be removed from the lower floor trash room almost at will. This was another reason why it was recommended that the metal door to the trash chute remain locked inside the computer room.

A study of the building plans in a West Coast **The dumbwaiter** computer center reflected that at one time there had been a dumbwaiter between the ground floor and other floors of the building. An examination of this construction feature revealed that the open shaft had been permanently sealed off at the ceiling of the second floor, where the computer was located, and that the dumbwaiter was no longer in operation. The shaft was still open, however, between the lower terminal in a first floor closet and the second floor terminal inside the computer room.

A possibility here was that an agile individual or a person with a ladder could utilize the open shaft to climb up into the computer room. And as in the case of the trash chute, a fire beginning on the first floor could easily spread into the computer room through this shaft. For these reasons it was recommended that the dumbwaiter shaft be sealed structurally.

Ceiling crawl space

A study of building plans frequently reveals that the computer room or tape library can be entered through the ceiling crawl space. In these cases it may be a relatively simple matter for an intruder to push up on ceiling tiles in rooms adjoining the computer room or library. If interior walls do not extend all the way to the ceiling, entry can be made by lifting out ceiling tiles on the other side of the wall.

It is desirable for walls to be constructed so that there is no access through the crawl space; and if such access does exist, partitions should be extended upward. As an alternative, reasonable protection may be afforded by securing rolls of heavy, woven wire above those walls that are of inadequate height.

Air vents

It is sometimes possible for an intruder to enter a computer room or tape library by crawling through air conditioning vents. Ducts or vents of this kind usually originate in a mechanical room, where the presence of an intruder may not be as readily noted as in some other areas.

Some vents are so small that they will not allow entry. Right-angle turns in other ducts may make them unusable to an intruder. If penetration through vents is possible, however, it is suggested that heavy-duty steel grills be adequately secured over access openings.

Computer library doors

It is sometimes observed that adequate locks have been provided for computer room doors, but that no lock of any kind has been placed on the tape library door. This is on the idea that a tape librarian is on duty there on a twenty-four-hour basis (three shifts), and that the library is never unattended.

This kind of thinking ignores the possibility that it may be necessary to evacuate the entire building in the event of a fire, bomb threat, or other emergency. If a lock is provided, and it is necessary to leave the building, then tapes stored inside the library would still be reasonably secure against theft or sabotage when the library was unattended.

As a precaution, it is suggested that the lock on the tape library door should be openable from the inside, to preclude the possibility that an employee could be locked inside.

It is also recommended that there be an automatic closing device on the tape library door, that would be activated in the event of fire, even though employees should leave the building.

The forklift

A forklift is often used at a computer center in loading paper supplies and equipment. Unless properly controlled, this equipment can be very dangerous from a security standpoint.

A forklift may conceivably be used to pick up a safe containing backup tapes and lift the safe into a pickup truck at a loading dock. The forklift might also be used by militants to break open some data safes or locked cabinets, making use of the heavy forks on the lift. In addition, it could be used to break open the library walls, especially if those walls were constructed of sheetrock or wooden materials.

If it is possible to garage the forklift in a separate, lockable building, it is suggested that this be done. In addition, it is recommended that keys to this piece of equipment be carefully controlled by the personnel authorized to use the forklift.

Decorating

Management has an obligation to provide pleasant work surroundings, but it is suggested that painting and decorating be kept to a minimum in the computer room. Whenever used, wallpaper, carpeting, and paints should be fire-resistant.

A large eastern corporation recently redecorated a large administrative building that included the company computer installation. To improve the corporate image the executive vice president of this firm ordered all hallways in the building carpeted and all walls covered with wallpaper. Tests of carpeting in areas of the building near the computer room revealed that this floor covering had not been treated for surface flammability, and that it burned readily.

Alarm systems

There are so many kinds of protection that may be afforded by alarm systems that the advice of a loss prevention consultant is recommended in this regard.

Check off list

1.
Is the computer building isolated from other structures, so that intruders will be more readily observed, and so that the building will be isolated from fire?

2.
Are plantings of shrubbery and trees kept a reasonable distance from the building?

3.
Is night lighting adequate?

4.
Is fencing needed? Adequate? Properly installed?

5.
Is key control such that unauthorized persons are not allowed to obtain keys?

6.
Are walls of solid masonry, where possible?

7.
Are unnecessary windows bricked up or covered with heavy steel mesh, properly secured to the building?

8.
Have unnecessary breaks in the building wall been eliminated?

9.
Are there trash chutes, coal chutes, or dumbwaiter shafts that allow access to the computer room or tape library?

10.

Is it possible to enter sensitive computer areas through the ceiling crawl space?

11.

Is computer access possible through air conditioning vents?

12.

Is there a lock on the tape library door?

13.

Is the forklift at the computer center kept under control?

14.

Are alarm systems designed by individuals with professional experience?

4

THE THREAT OF FIRE

Modern Electronic Data Processing, however helpful, is nevertheless a serious fire hazard.

The business development that resulted from the invention of the computer has been characterized as the most phenomenal growth industry of all time. During the course of this development, old-style paper records were replaced by the singularly abbreviated forms used in the computer—magnetized tapes and discs.

At first it was not realized that there were critical differences between the protection requirements of paper records and these new tapes and discs. But it was soon apparent that the new records were very sensitive to fire damage.

It was also learned by bitter experience that there are a number of characteristics of an EDP center that make it unusually vulnerable to fire.

As a result of these factors, the threat of fire continues to be the most feared environmental risk to the present-day computer.

Differences between EDP records and paper

Paper documents may continue to be legible until exposed to temperatures of about 350°F. At higher temperatures they become a charred, blackened mass. Modern fire safes for the protection of paper business records generally make use of insulating materials containing gypsum plaster or other hydrous compounds. When subjected to fire, these insulating materials are changed chemically, giving off steam that protects papers in the safe without seriously harming the contents.

But this type of protection is not suitable for computer records. While the self-ignition temperature of polyester-backed tape is around 1,000°F., heat and humidity may cause damage at temperatures well below that point. In the first place, tests indicate that continued exposure to temperatures no higher than 150°F. may cause tapes to be unreadable.

Water, in itself, causes no damage to tapes over a short period of time; but humidity levels in excess of

85 percent can be expected to ruin magnetic tapes at temperatures no greater than 150°F., or as low as 130°F. Steam, which results when water is sprayed on fire, may ruin computer tapes. In relying on old-style business safes to protect computer records, it was found that losses resulted, since the hydrous compounds making up the insulating materials in the walls of the safe were converted into steam.

As soon as fire safes designed to protect paper records were found unsuitable for computer requirements, new types of safes were placed on the market by safe manufacturers. A comparison of protection requirements is shown in Illustration 4.

A photograph of a modern data safe appears in Illustration 5 on the following page.

There are a number of characteristics that make an EDP center vulnerable to fire. The systems involved draw considerable amounts of electrical power. In an installation of almost any size there will be a veritable maze of wires and electrical connections in the area under the floor. If one of these circuits "shorts out," it may continue to overheat and spread intense fire.

Then too, leading authorities on fire protection and computer room security state that there is no such thing as a completely fireproof building. Actual cases show that floor-to-floor integrity originally designed into a structure is frequently lost by holes broken through masonry walls and floors for the installation of electrical conduits and telephone connections. A program to seal these openings should be part of a computer security program, since these holes serve as "chimneys" for the spread of building fire and "drains" for the spread of flood water.

Fire-prone characteristics of computer centers

And regardless of the building construction, there are frequently considerable quantities of combustibles in the machine room—furniture, curtains, floor coverings, paper stocks and supplies, plastic containers, punch cards, and writing materials. In addition, components, accessories, and equipment associated with computers will often support com-

	Paper record safes	EDP record safes
Temperatures at which records begin to deteriorate	350°	150°
Permissible humidity levels	Any	85% maximum
Construction features	Single safe construction with single insulating qualities	A safe-within-a-safe with insulating properties
Interior design	Maximum flexibility to accommodate ordinary files, records and paper	Maximum flexibility to enable storage of a variety of EDP information record media (e.g. tapes, discs, microfilm, etc.)

Illustration 4.
Comparison of protection afforded by paper record safes and EDP record safes

Illustration 5.
A modern data safe

bustion. The insulation from electrical wiring, circuit cards, cable insulation, hydraulic oil, plastic filters from air conditioners, wood-framed partitions, and wall decorations are only some of the materials of this kind.

Fires in an EDP center frequently originate in areas that cannot be readily seen—under the raised flooring, in equipment cabinets, or in the area under drop ceilings. An overheated electrical connection, for example, may smolder under the raised floor for a long period. When the problem is eventually discovered and a floor panel (tile) is removed to get at the fire, fumes may immediately flare out, filling the room with gas and smoke. These gases may choke computer room employees and seriously obstruct visibility. Computer components, plastic items, and cable coverings often give off a toxic, heavy smoke while burning. In a small, confined room, this outpouring of fumes may make it very difficult to approach the blaze.

In addition, deliberately setting a fire may be one of the most logical methods of attack available to anyone bent on destroying a computer or seriously harming a business.

In the early development of EDP, little study was given to the possibility of computer fires.

Major computer fires

The U.S. Department of Defense (Pentagon building) fire of July 2, 1959, was one of the most widely known examples of fire loss. Damage occurred in a 4,000-square-foot area in the computer room of the Air Force Statistical Division offices, reportedly when a 300-watt bulb overheated a fire-resistant ceiling in a basement room. Three IBM computers and between 5,000 and 7,000 tapes were lost when the blaze swept through the computer room and the tape library. The spread of the fire was influenced by combustible partitions, concealed spaces containing wood framing, combustible supplies, and suspended ceilings that burned. Loss to the government was estimated at $6.69 million.

The Pentagon fire served as a warning to other

Illustration 6.
Photograph of the Phelps Dodge Copper Company building, Fort Wayne, Indiana, in which 150 tapes were protected by data safe, August 1966

installations, and fire protection firms continued to develop new types of fire detectors and supressants. Meanwhile, manufacturers in the record protection industry developed new types of safes for safeguarding nonpaper records.

The Phelps Dodge Copper Company explosion at Fort Wayne, Indiana, in August 1966 was a landmark case in the protection of computer records. In that incident a Honeywell H-200 leased system and associated equipment was completely destroyed in the explosion. About 150 magnetic tape files of considerable value were saved, however, because they had been stored in a newly developed type of fireproof and explosionproof safe.

The Phelps Dodge data processing manager subsequently was quoted as saying, "We bought that safe two years ago and thought it was a big white elephant."[1]

[1] William S. Bates, "Security of Computer-Based Information Systems," *Datamation*, May 1970, p. 64. Reprinted with permission of *Datamation*, copyright Technical Publishing Co., Greenwich, CT, 06830, 1970.

Oxygen, fuel, and a means of ignition must be present for a fire to break out. Oxygen-carrying air is almost always in plentiful supply in computer operating areas, due to the common use of air conditioning systems in maintaining desirable operating temperatures. After students set fire to the computer room at California State University at Fresno, during May 1970, the manager of the computer installation recommended the installation of master (panic) switches near all room exits. The reason given for the installation of these switches was to override the air conditioner switch, and thus reduce the amount of available oxygen.[2]

As has already been pointed out, fuel may be available in a computer installation in the form of readout paper, punch cards, unused paper supplies, accumulated trash, cable insulation, and plastic materials.

Ignition may originate from employee cigarettes, unless there is a strict prohibition against smoking. In one recent instance, a fire started when an employee dropped a smoldering cigarette through a floor cable entrance opening. Accumulated lunch bags, crumpled cigarette packages, and trash that had been discarded under the raised floor were ignited by the cigarette. Other computer room fires have been attributed to faulty electrical equipment, malfunctioning mechanical devices, combustible materials that were ignited by an incandescent lamp, soldering or welding equipment, faulty air conditioning pumps, fluorescent lamp ballasts, and overhead resistors.

Electrical wires and cables are, of course, installed under raised floors in most computer locations. In some very small installations, cables may be left on top of the working floor or installed in overhead troughs.

Raised floors, including the structural supporting

[2] "Fire Bombs Damage a Computer Center," *The Office*, August 1970, p. 43.

members, are normally of aluminum, steel, concrete, or noncombustible composition materials. In most instances, access panels (tiles or sections) are readily removable, so that all space beneath is accessible. From a fire prevention standpoint, it is important that openings in raised floors be screened or protected to prevent the accumulation of debris beneath the raised floor. It is also suggested that a regular program be set up for cleaning the underfloor area.

It is also recommended that metal floors be grounded, so that the supporting members will not act as carriers of electricity in the event of a short circuit.

It is taken for granted by computer room personnel that great numbers of electrical cables are used in the installation. Some members of management, however, express surprise on observing the concentration of underfloor cables that are needed. Illustration 7 shows cables in a typical computer installation under an operating room floor.

Available statistics on computer fires reflect that a good number of EDP fires originate in the area under the raised floor. At any rate, the tightly grouped electrical cables constitute a serious hazard, due to the density of spacing and the electrical current that may short-circuit. Most of these cables are covered with flame-retardant materials and so-called self-extinguishing insulation and jackets. Some cables are metal jacketed, while others may be protected with a thermoplastic jacket or polyvinyl chloride.

Basic protection requirements

A basic program for protection against business or institutional fires requires three elements:

1. Steps to prevent the outbreak of fire;
2. Steps to prevent the serious spread of fire; and
3. Procedures for the prompt (a) detection and (b) extinguishment of fire.

Because of the possibility of human or mechanical failure, it is unsafe to place sole reliance on any one of these basic elements.

Illustration 7.
Photographs showing the
density of underfloor
cables in a typical
computer room

Preventing fires　　　　Good housekeeping practices can be expected to prevent many computer room fires. Rules should be formulated by supervision and frequently checked to insure compliance.

As a practical matter, however, a computer security consultant usually finds that management sets up proper programs and controls, but frequently fails to supervise the implementation of them. It is therefore emphasized that management should utilize a so-called "tickler file" or "come-up file," to be reminded to make necessary verification of all computer security procedures.

Suggested good housekeeping and engineering practices should include:

1. A rule against smoking in the computer room or tape library, as previously mentioned;
2. A procedure for the frequent removal of all waste or trash materials, with metal covers on the top of containers at all times;
3. A prohibition against storing paper stocks, unused punch cards, or other supplies in operating areas;
4. A rule against painting, soldering, welding, or bringing combustibles into the area while operations are in progress. Fire-resistant paint should be utilized;
5. A procurement policy for using noncombustible furniture, drapes, and furnishings throughout the computer system area and nearby storage rooms;
6. A procedure to de-energize all electrical equipment and computer systems when not attended, if practical;
7. A requirement that all electrical equipment and wiring be in accordance with approved codes. Transformers should be located outside the computer systems area, if possible.

An ideal　　　　In seeking to engineer an ideal fire extinguishing
extinguishing system　system, fire researchers have set four critical tests:

1. The system must quickly detect and promptly extinguish any fire,
2. The system must be safe—that is, people using the extinguishing agent must not be harmed thereby,
3. The system must be reasonable in cost and easy to install and maintain, and
4. The agent must leave no residue that may damage delicate equipment or costly objects, or create expensive cleanup problems.

Fire detectors

Fires, or conditions likely to produce fires, may be detected by the human senses. In most instances, however, automatic sensors or detectors are far more reliable and will usually give earlier warning. Then too, fire may begin in a computer area when no employees are at work there.

These detection devices will note the presence of smoke, heat, or flame, and can be relied on to activate an alarm system, or sound an audible noise, or to activate water sprinklers or gaseous extinguishing agents.

Perhaps the type of fire detectors most commonly used in commercial buildings are the so-called conventional thermal or "rate-of-rise" detectors. These devices trigger an alarm whenever there is a sudden increase in temperature. This kind of system is very dependable and is seldom subject to false alarms.

In actual practice, however, it has been found that some computer fires may burn for a considerable time without appreciably raising the temperature in the computer room. This is usually because computer installations make use of air conditioning systems that circulate large quantities of air, dissipating the heat from a localized fire. As a result, the fire may make considerable progress before temperature changes are sufficient to activate a rate-of-rise detector. For this reason, detectors that are sensitive to smoke and other products of combustion (ionization detectors) are to be preferred.

Ionization detectors are very sensitive and may be set off by chemical particles in minute quantities of smoke, dust particles, or by any change in the gaseous content of the air, as well as by unusual variations in air currents. Using some types of cleaning solvents, or smoking only one cigarette in the computer room may be sufficient to activate these ionization detectors. Fire experts are generally in agreement that it is preferable to set the sensitivity of ionization detectors so that they warn of computer equipment fires as early as possible; and when detectors are set for this kind of sensitivity, there is a possibility for false alarms.

The types of detectors specified for computers by the National Fire Protection Association are:

5501. Automatic fire detection equipment capable of detecting fire in the incipient stage shall be installed. The equipment used shall be listed products of combustion and/or smoke detection types. Each installation shall be engineered for the specific area to be protected giving due consideration to air currents and patterns within the space.[3]

In addition, the National Fire Protection Association has pointed out that smoke or fire detectors should be located in the areas under the floor, as well as in other locations, if the existing raised floor is combustible.

Some computer installations rely on an overhead water sprinkler system to put out fires, and ignore the installation of an independent fire detecting system. A water sprinkler system of this type is actuated by the melting of fusible links in the overhead sprinklers. One of the weaknesses in this system is that air conditioning currents may dissipate the heat generated by the fire. Consequently, floor level temperatures may be extremely hot before fusible links in the ceiling are melted.

---

[3] Reproduced by permission from the Standard for the Protection of Electronic Computer/Data Processing Equipment (NFPA No. 75), 1972 edition, copyright National Fire Protection Association, Boston, Mass.

Ideally, fire detectors should be installed at the inside top of each console. But in addition to providing protection for specific units, it is recommended that detectors be hung in ceiling areas, in exhaust and air return ducts, and in the underfloor areas as well. **Location of detectors**

Modern systems are available to indicate which specific fire detector has sensed the presence of smoke or products of combustion, and has activated the alarm. These systems usually light a numbered square on a control grid, showing the location of the fire and sounding an audible alarm. Some systems also sound an alarm at a central station of a commercial alarm company. By looking at the grid, an employee or fire fighter can proceed to the direct location of the alarm with a hand extinguisher, ascertain whether there is a fire, and put it out if the blaze is still localized.

There are three types of fixed fire extinguishing systems regularly used in computer installations to put out fire after it has been detected. These are: **Extinguishing agents**

1. Automatic water sprinkler systems,
2. Carbon dioxide systems, and
3. Halogenated extinguishing agent systems, utilizing halon 1301 (known by the DuPont trade name "Freon").

Dry chemical extinguishants and high-expansion foam have also been used in infrequent situations.

In the past, no system for extinguishing fires in commercial installations has been so widely used as the automatic (water) sprinkler system. Installed in business or industrial buildings of all types, this system makes use of an arrangement of water-filled pipes in the ceiling that release water through sprinkler heads when a preset temperature (generally about 160°F. to 180°F.) is reached. Once started, this flow of water will continue indefinitely until shut off manually. To prevent unnecessary water damage, as well as to notify the fire department that there is a fire, a system of this kind is frequently connected with an alarm system that sounds at the **Water** central station of a commercial alarm company or local fire department headquarters.

Local building and fire codes require the use of sprinkler systems in some localities, and insurance companies sometimes specify this type of extinguishing system.

There are a number of advantages to a water sprinkler installation, but there are also some serious drawbacks. Comparatively, it is inexpensive to install and maintain. In a serious fire, there is a continuous stream of water as long as necessary. Then too, water cools off the fire, so that it will not "flash back," or continue to burst into flame as soon as application of the extinguishing agent has stopped. In addition, this type of installation is usually trouble free and reliable in operation.

But the use of water as an extinguishing agent may cause some severe problems. In the first place, water from an overhead sprinkler cannot be expected to reach a fire inside a computer equipment cabinet.

Then too, steam almost invariably results when water from a sprinkler head strikes a fire. While tape will probably withstand temperatures of 250°F. or perhaps even 300°F. in a dry environment, the introduction of water can be expected to seriously lower the damage tolerance of computer tape.

It has been found to be very important that the electrical power to the computer be turned off at the time water strikes a fire. Unless the power is off, serious damage may be done to the computer system, apparently after water has caused short circuits in electrical connections.

In instances where sprinkler heads may be activated before the fire is discovered by computer room personnel, a method for automatic detection is recommended, that will automatically cut off electronic components as soon as possible.

If there is no automatic method for de-energizing computer equipment when sprinkler heads are activated, it is important for operating personnel to immediately cut off the power by means of an emergency cutoff (panic) switch.

Some modern computer installations utilize sensitive detection equipment with a "dry pipe" installation. This delays discharge of the water supply through previously uncharged lines, allowing an employee to delay water flow until it is apparent that a false alarm is not involved. An additional advantage here is that accidental breakage of one sprinkler head will not likely cause flooding, as in "wet pipe" or "charged pipe" sprinkler systems.

Then too, water from charged lines usually contains conductive sediments that cause short-circuit paths in the computer system. The flow from a dry pipe installation usually contains far less conductive impurities in the water. It is these conductive sediments that may cause serious problems. At best, computer equipment would need to be dried out thoroughly before being repowered and used again.

But if computer equipment was de-energized prior to the water flooding, then the only problem may be that of cleanup. In several known cases of this kind, recovery was accomplished by draining away surface water, and by using large blowers and dehumidifiers. Time may be of great importance here—it is essential that water be promptly removed.

As another precaution here, experience indicates that water sprinkler systems protecting computer rooms should preferably be valved separately from other sprinkler systems in the same building. It is also essential that an adequate drainage system be located in the underfloor area.

During the Christmas season in 1972, a serious fire broke out in a California State Office building at Sacramento, California, causing damage in excess of several million dollars. This building housed computers operated by the state Motor Vehicle Department. The fire activated a water sprinkler system and a considerable quantity of water was discharged into the computer room. This installation was not in operation at the time, but employees had followed a procedure of covering computer equipment with plastic covers.

The protection afforded by these plastic covers reduced water loss to a minimum. This technique may, of course, have application in other computer installations that do not operate on a three-shift basis.

The approach here is that a fire occurring under the cover would almost immediately burn away the plastic, allowing the water discharge to reach the burning area. Other equipment would remain covered against water damage.

This protective measure requires a few minutes at the end of the second shift to place covers on equipment. In the California incident, at least, the time was well justified.

Photos of the California State Office building and of the interior of the computer room appear in Illustrations 8 and 9.

In experimenting with extinguishing agents other than water, it was found that some dry chemical agents were very effective on electrical fires of the type common to EDP installations. Use of these agents has been generally abandoned, however, since it was found that the dry chemical agents leave a microscopic residue on computer components that may be as harmful to the computer as the fire itself.

Experiments have also been made with high-expansion foam flooding systems. Since this material makes use of a water base, it seems to have the same disadvantages as water. As a conductor of electricity, high-expansion foam should be applied only after the computer has been de-energized. In addition, the foam has a tendency to drift away or pile up in certain areas of the room that is to be protected. The coverage afforded is therefore not uniform. For these reasons, little consideration is now being given to high-expansion foam as an extinguishing agent.

Carbon dioxide (CO_2) flooding systems came into use in computer installations because of the problems associated with water sprinkler systems. In the first place, carbon dioxide does not corrode computer terminals or ruin sensitive equipment. Operation may be resumed as soon as the fire is out and the carbon dioxide has been blown away. It also mixes well with the air, not tending to pile up or protect only certain areas of a room. In addition, it is not a conductor of electricity, and there is no requirement that equipment be de-energized before application.

It should be emphasized, however, that carbon dioxide is a deadly gas, especially in the concentrations that will be needed in an enclosed computer room. Carbon dioxide should never be installed without first training computer room personnel in the dangers that may be involved. And at least some employees should be qualified in the use of a self-contained breathing apparatus (not a mere gas mask).

Because of the dangerous nature of this gas, it is always necessary to sound an alarm prior to discharge, so that employees can make their way out of the danger area. This delay also allows additional time for the fire to spread.

Another factor here is that a carbon dioxide system cannot continue to discharge indefinitely, like a water sprinkler system. When the available supply of carbon dioxide is exhausted, other fire fighting resources must be used. Rapid extinguishment, as supplied by a carbon dioxide or by a halon (Freon) system, may not always cool down the burning material as efficiently as does water. Therefore, there may be re-ignition of the heated substances in the fire area when gaseous extinguishants such as carbon dioxide or halon (Freon) have been dissipated. Also, it can be expected that the installation of a carbon dioxide system will be more expensive than a water installation.

In addition, the discharge of carbon dioxide in

Illustration 8.
California State Office
building on fire,
December 26, 1972

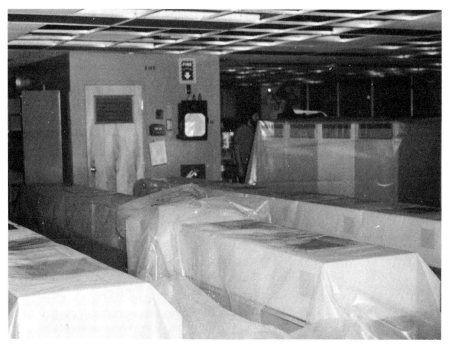

Illustration 9.
Electronic equipment
protected by plastic
covers—California State
Office building,
December 26, 1972

strength immediately clouds the atmosphere, so that it is impossible to see at all. This condition may add an additional element of danger, as an employee trapped in the computer room after the discharge of gas might not be able to find his way out before being overcome. This lack of visibility also hampers rescue efforts, as well as concealing the location of the fire.

Halon (Freon)

The most important concern of any business is the protection of its employees. The known dangers of carbon dioxide caused the development and marketing of a series of halogenated extinguishing agents that pose far less danger to computer room personnel. The best-known extinguishing agent in this group is halon 1301, commonly known by the trade name "Freon," under which it is marketed by the manufacturer, the Du Pont Corporation.

Exactly how halon puts out a fire is not known, but it is believed that this is by a chemical action on the combustion process itself, so that there is no further burning. Halon is an odorless, clear gas that does not conduct electricity and does not leave any residue that would harm electrical equipment. It must, however, be mixed into the air in the proper proportion, as it is considerably heavier than air. Therefore, the discharge system must be properly planned and installed.

Photographs of halon discharge equipment, and a sketch of a halon total flooding system appear in Illustrations 10 and 11.

While halon 1301, in itself is not corrosive, some of the products of decombustion that occur during certain fires may corrode some of the materials in a computer system. The extent of this possibility has not been completely determined.

While halon 1301 does not present as high a degree of danger as carbon dioxide, halon 1301 is nevertheless a toxic substance. Discharge concentrations of greater than 15 percent should not be used where there is any chance of human exposure.

There have been no reported deaths from exposure to halon 1301. The National Fire Protection Association has noted, however, that there are no appreciable effects on humans at concentrations below 7 percent for exposure up to 5 minutes. "At concentrations of 7 to 10 percent effects such as dizziness, impaired coordination, and reduced mental acuity become definite with exposures of a few minutes' duration; . . . At concentrations of the order of 15 to 20 percent, there is the risk of unconsciousness and possibly death if the exposure is prolonged."[4]

Some tests show that burning wood cribs and wooden pallets were readily extinguished with a discharge of less than 5 percent halon 1301 that was maintained for less than 10 minutes. However, discharge requirements for deep-seated fires are considerably greater. If the fire involves smoldering combustion, not subject to immediate extinguishment as in flaming combustion, then neither halon 1301 nor carbon dioxide may be adequate to prevent re-ignition. Flaming combustion in solid fuels, however, is promptly extinguished by low concentrations of halon 1301.

Halon 1301 total flooding systems have considerable value in computer room applications, but available information indicates their effectiveness will usually be limited to fires in solid combustibles which can be extinguished before they become deep seated. In common with carbon dioxide, halon 1301 has a limited supply of extinguishing gas, and the fire may "flash back" after the supply of gas has been exhausted.

It is also to be noted that halon systems are more expensive in most instances than water sprinkler installations or than those of carbon dioxide.

Regardless of the efficiency and reliability of sprinkler or total gaseous flooding systems, it is rec-

Hand fire extinguishers

[4] Reproduced by permission from the Standard on Halogenated Extinguishing Agent Systems—Halon 1301 (NFPA No. 12A), 1972 edition, copyright National Fire Protection Association, Boston, Mass.

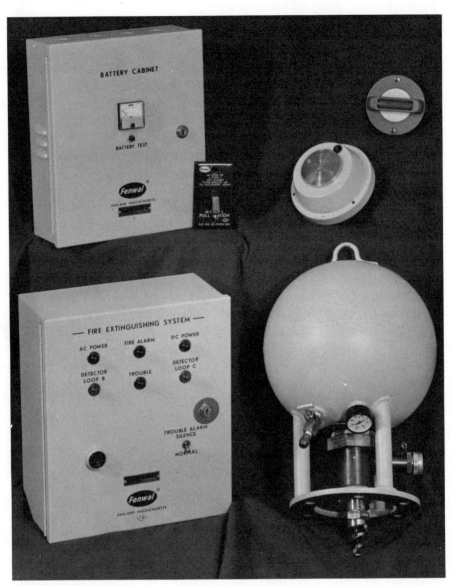

Illustration 10.
Halon (Freon) discharge
equipment, for a total
flooding system

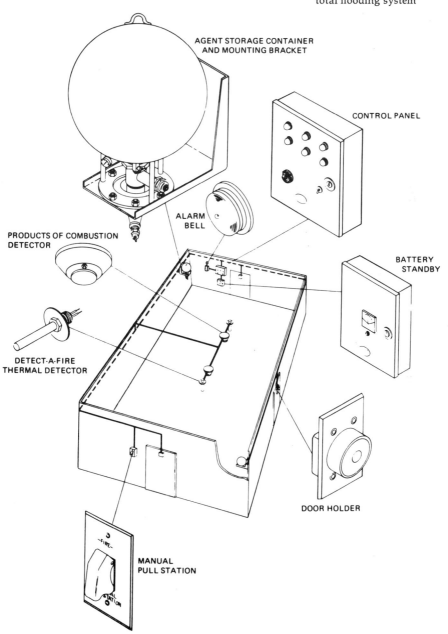

Illustration 11.
Sketch of a halon (Freon)
total flooding system

AGENT STORAGE CONTAINER
AND MOUNTING BRACKET

CONTROL PANEL

ALARM
BELL

PRODUCTS OF COMBUSTION
DETECTOR

BATTERY
STANDBY

DETECT-A-FIRE
THERMAL DETECTOR

DOOR HOLDER

MANUAL
PULL STATION

ommended that hand fire extinguishers be available throughout the entire computer installation. At least some of these extinguishers should be capable of combating an electrical fire; and all extinguishers should be clearly marked as to the type of fires for which they were designed.

It is also suggested that any hand extinguisher selected should be equipped with a nozzle or hose arrangement that can be readily inserted under the raised floor.

Another good loss prevention practice involves hanging all hand extinguishers on hooks or mounting brackets where they are easily available, and the absence of an extinguisher would be immediately noticed. Painted "targets" of a distinctive color on the wall or support behind each extinguisher bracket will insure immediate location of the nearest apparatus in case of emergency.

A regular program to have extinguishers checked for serviceability would appear to be an obvious precaution.

It is not unusual for an inexperienced individual utilizing a hand extinguishers to scatter glowing sparks and ash material over a wide area. This is especially so when an extinguisher is discharged into a wire mesh trash basket that contains a fire. It is for this reason that wire mesh containers are not recommended for use in a computer installation.

In numerous instances it has been reported that employees fighting fires in a computer installation were inadequately trained in the operation of hand extinguishers. Fire prevention authorities therefore recommend that a number of key individuals on all shifts be given training in putting out fires under supervised conditions. Some practical training of this type is sometimes available through local fire departments or through commercial concerns that refill hand extinguishers.

Protecting the remainder of the building

Good fire protection should extend to all areas of the building, not to the computer installation alone. If water sprinkler systems are used throughout the remainder of the building, it is recommended that water sprinkler valves for these areas should be secured by a chain and padlock in an "on" position. This, of course, should not be done without the approval of the fire insurance company.

While water damage could result if there was an accidental breakage of a sprinkler head, it is usually preferable to take the calculated risk of shutting off the system in a hurry. The alternative here is that a vandal could turn off the system when no one was around and thereafter set fire to the building. If the sprinkler valve is locked in an "on" position, adequate provision should be made to keep keys to the lock readily available. A contact with the local fire department is also recommended, to ascertain that the locking arrangement is not in violation of fire ordinances.

A technique that has been used by militants in an effort to hinder firemen has involved stuffing trash, sticks, soft drink bottles, and debris into fire hose standpipes located on the outside of the building under attack. Vandalism of this kind can be observed by regular inspections by building maintenance employees. If militant action against a computer installation appears to be a possibility, it is suggested that regular examinations of this kind be continued.

1.
Has a definite plan for fire protection been formulated?

2.
Are all employees aware of protection requirements and individual responsibilities in case of fire?

3.
Are paper forms and supplies kept to a minimum in the operating room?

4.
Do all floors, walls, ceilings, and construction features have fire-resistant qualities?

5.

Has drainage of water from floors above been sealed off so that water will not drain into the computer room in case of fire?

6.

Are electrical cables and fixtures covered with flame-retardant materials and so-called self-extinguishing insulation or jackets?

7.

Are "floor pullers" readily available so that floor tiles can be easily removed to get at the location of an underfloor fire? Is the location of floor pullers properly marked and are they retained in the assigned location?

8.

Are rules against smoking in the computer room and the tape library strictly enforced?

9.

Are trash and waste materials frequently removed from operating areas?

10.

Do maintenance employees understand that there should be a prohibition against painting, soldering, welding, or storing of combustibles in operating areas?

11.

Are drapes, chairs, desks, storage cabinets, and furnishings of noncombustible materials? What about curtains and rugs?

12.

Are all pieces of electronic equipment de-energized when not attended?

13.

Do employees understand that they should immediately de-energize equipment in the event water is to be used to put out a fire?

14.

Are electrical transformers located ontside computer areas?

15.

Have heat, smoke, or flame detectors been installed to detect fire? Have they been located under the floor? Inside the false ceiling? Inside specific units?

16.

Has consideration been given to installation of a water sprinkler or halon 1301 system for total flooding been considered?

17.

Do employees understand how to use fire extinguishers?

18.

Is a self-contained breathing apparatus available to rescue someone overcome by carbon dioxide or halon?

19.

If carbon dioxide is used, do employees understand the dangers? Are they appropriately warned prior to discharge?

20.

Are water sprinkler systems in a computer area on a separate system from the remainder of the building?

21.

Are sufficient hand extinguishers available? Are at least some of these extinguishers of the type that can be used on an electrical fire?

22.

Is the safe used to store computer tapes or disks the type that will protect tapes or disks?

23.

Is there good drainage under the computer room floor?

24.

Would plastic sheets protect computers from water damage?

5

COMPUTER SYSTEMS AND CONTINGENCY PLANNING

If many of the employee functions are dependent on the operation of the computer, then a firm can ill afford even a temporary operational shutdown. Business may come to a halt, for example, if daily orders and reports are not made, inventory figures are not available, and accounts receivable cannot be verified.

Yet it is undisputed that all mechanical devices may eventually fail. As one writer on computer protection put it, "Provision should be made in advance for hardware failure, which is inevitable in the operation of any computer system."[1]

While it is usually a secondary consideration, the heavy cash investment or lease expense may be another compelling argument to keep equipment in operating condition at all times. Computer downtime can be very expensive. Insistence on adherence to approved operating techniques will help to insure continued machine operation.

The procedures that may be indicated when a failure occurs may vary with the type of equipment and its use in the operation. An effective planning approach should include an appraisal of each individual piece of equipment and the effects of its failure in the overall processing system.

It is suggested that this evaluation consider the consequences of each component's failure, followed by laying out a plan for an alternate method of processing. Under some circumstances, management could revert to the prior system of manual operations; but all too often it is found that employees no longer have the training or available hours that would be required for manual processing.

There may be times when a substitute may be made for a peripheral unit that has become inopera-

[1] Richard A. Levine, "How to Protect Your EDP Records," *New York Certified Public Accountant*, May 1969, p. 354.

tive. For example, if a line printer on the system "goes down," it may be possible to use magnetic tape as temporary storage for output of programs that would normally be printed on the line printer. When the line printer is repaired, the output stored on the magnetic tape can be output to the line printer. In cases of this kind it is suggested that this alternative be documented as part of operations procedures.

Not only does each piece of equipment need evaluation, but the requirements of the whole system should be examined. Dependable alternate sources of electrical power and air conditioning are frequently an absolute necessity.

Of course, the obvious solution to some breakdowns would be to have duplicate hardware on hand. Because of cost this is prohibitive in most instances. A firm that operates six delivery trucks may find it feasible to maintain seven vehicles, utilizing a spare when regular vehicles break down or need periodic overhauls. But few firms can even consider the cost of a spare computer.

Duplicate hardware

There are times, however, when it may be advisable to purchase or lease some extra equipment. A computer application that requires three tape drives for running should consider having a fourth as part of the configuration for protection against failure. In any event, an equipment feasibility study should balance the need for backup equipment with the requirements of financial reality.

Redundancy of at least some equipment may be a desirable objective. But if the backup machine is located in the same computer room as the original, then the secondary device also will frequently be useless because of the same disaster or shortage of electrical power that crippled the principal hardware.

In considering essential requirements for emergency computer operation, it is also suggested that plans include a responsible management team prepared to handle computer operations if it should

A management backup team

become absolutely necessary. This recommendation applies especially to firms that have union-organized EDP employees. It is also important that approved security procedures continue in force, even if emergency personnel must be used.

Backup electrical power

The operation of the computer center relies heavily on closely controlled temperature and humidity, as well as the continued supply of electric power.

Americans generally assume that cheap and abundant electrical energy will always be available. As the power to light and heat buildings, propel cars and planes, operate computers and other machinery, electricity is an essential part of our industrial society. Yet critical shortages in electrical power may be a reality in the immediate future. Information released by the Petroleum Industry Research Foundation reflects that the nation's energy consumption from 1965 to 1971 rose about 5 percent a year, or more than four times as fast as the population of the United States.

Time magazine summarized the possibilities of this problem:

What ever became of the great energy shortage? Only a few months ago, headlines spouted warnings that a pinch on fuel supplies might force winter power blackouts or brownouts . . . the shortage was not so much averted as postponed. Fuel supplies were adequate only because the General Motors strike and the economic recession limited industrial demand for power. . . . In some future winter of business boom and bitter cold—or future summer of blistering heat that balloons air conditioning demand—the U.S. is almost sure to face the same threat again.[2]

Unless generating capacity is increased, it seems likely that there may be other shortages like the great northeastern power blackout of November 1965. The U.S. Federal Power Commission reported

[2]"Getting More Power to the People," *Time*, April 19, 1971, p. 72. Reprinted by permission from *Time*, the Weekly Newsmagazine, copyright Time, Inc.

97 major power failures in 1967 alone, scattered from Alaska to Massachusetts.

Hurricanes, lightning storms, and other severe weather conditions were responsible for approximately 31 percent of the power failures in recent years. Large parts of the Texas Gulf Coast area were without electricity for six days following hurricane "Beulah."

Even if a major disaster does not cause a lengthy power outage, a short power failure can cause damage to the data processing function. Loss of data stored in the computer main memory or possible damage to magnetic discs, drums, or tapes can occur in a surprise power outage. If the data processing function is sufficiently critical it may be advisable to explore having available a temporary power source that is sufficient to allow for an orderly shutdown of the computer system when a commercial power outage occurs. Many temporary power sources are available commercially. Most of these units are designed to provide power for the computer from storage batteries. Due to the large power consumption of a computer system and its peripheral equipment, the batteries usually provide power for only a short period of time, normally less than one-half hour. However, in a matter of minutes the operation of most computer systems can be stopped without damage to equipment or data.

Often, power failures occur on the power substation level or in the distribution system from the substation to the user. In urban areas, it may be possible to arrange to receive power from two separate power substations and install automatic power switching equipment between the two power sources. In this way, if a power outage occurs on the power substation level of one power source, the equipment can be switched without interruption to the power source that is still functioning.

If continued operation of the computer system in times of a commercial power outage is mandatory, then it is necessary to provide a standby electrical generation capability. Major EDP installation needs may range from a diesel auxiliary generator costing in excess of $50,000, to more than $1 million for the backup power systems used by major airlines for their computerized ticket reservations.

Some major banks have installed diesel generators, locating the machinery in the concrete building, and protecting the fuel supply in underground storage tanks in areas patrolled by armed guards.

Backup air conditioning

The firm's management should realize that the EDP room air conditioning unit must have sufficient capacity, or the computer may cease to function. It is therefore important that the unit should be regularly maintained and serviced. An independent air conditioning backup is also recommended. If there is no backup source for emergency electrical power, however, all air conditioning units could be rendered useless.

Many companies have located emergency air conditioning ducts in the computer room, arranging to divert cool air from other parts of the building in the event of an emergency.

An unusually large computer installation in the South utilizes the city water supply to operate an air conditioning unit outside the main building. However, an unforeseen stoppage of the water supply would lead to a breakdown of the air conditioning. To forestall this possibility, the firm has arranged to put water from the bed of an adjoining river into the air conditioning tank. The river water may be polluted and unfit for human consumption at times, but it is adequate to keep the air conditioning unit in operation.

Foreseeing a simliar need, other firms have located water tanks on the premises, maintaining a backup supply of water to operate air conditioning systems.

Backup computer systems

It is to the credit of computer manufacturers that they seem to regard disaster as a particular challenge, expending unusual time and effort to put the disaster victim back into operation as quickly as possible.

Backup equipment is usually difficult to obtain, and replacement is needed rapidly. The length of time required for replacement will vary with the model and configuration of the machine, the computer manufacturer, and the business firm's influence with the manufacturer. In some instances it will be found that the computer in question is no longer made, although a secondhand model may be available. An appreciable amount of time may elapse prior to the replacement of even a single unit, not taking into account the others that may have been destroyed.

Under some other circumstances, the computer may be inoperable because of a mechanical breakdown or an extended interruption of electrical power or air conditioning. Under such circumstances a backup facility is needed to continue operations. Concerned management should make certain that such an emergency facility continues to be available.

All too often, as pointed out by Professor Brandt Allen, management has unrealistic ideas in this regard:

. . . when a senior executive of a major New England corporation was asked about the company's contingency plan, should its computer go down, he immediately replied that a nearby center could and would be used. A later interview with the manager of the center in question revealed that his center's equipment is not compatible with the company's; the nearest compatible equipment is located several hundred miles away; and that equipment is busy 24 hours a day, 7 days a week![3]

In commenting on this situation, one observer pointed out that "In my opinion, management's

[3] Brandt Allen, "Danger Ahead! Safeguard Your Computer," *Harvard Business Review*, November–December 1968, p. 98.

calm assurance that compatible backup facilities will be available during crises verges on suicidal myopia."[4]

When questioned regarding compatibility, businessmen will sometimes state that they are relying on a computer located in a nearby business house. Upon investigation, however, it will sometimes be found that the neighboring business has changed to another model computer.

Others may point out that "I am relying on the computer manufacturer to locate compatible equipment when I need it. After all, we spend considerable money with that manufacturer, and the computer representative has quite a bit of leverage with other EDP installations."

In other instances, the businessman may state that he belongs to the same lodge or club with a friend whose firm has a computer like that of the businessman. The latter may not have stopped to consider that his own company utilizes their computer in excess of 16 hours a day, and that the other firm has only a few free hours each week.

Even if two computers are the same model from the same manufacturer, there is no guarantee that a program that runs on one system can run on the other system. System configurations vary extensively, depending on the peripheral equipment, main memory size, and central processor options. Even if two systems have identical hardware, differences in the system software may make it impossible for the same program to run on both systems without modifications. There can be no guarantee of true compatibility without actual test runs at the backup facility. These are to be recommended in all cases. Since equipment changes can be anticipated in many companies, it is suggested that tests be repeated at regular intervals, if management is to continue to rely on the backup facility.

[4] Haig G. Neville, "Letter to the Editor," *Harvard Business Review*, May–June 1969, p. 40.

As an additional precaution, it is suggested that a written reciprocal agreement (cross-servicing agreement) be signed by officials of both companies that are involved in an arrangement to exchange backup facilities. This, of course, is a formal contract, and it is suggested the agreement be approved by the firms' attorneys prior to execution. A backup arrangement with several users of similar equipment would be even better.

Unless a firm is willing to take these precautions, experience shows that an understanding concerning a backup facility may be nothing more than a paper plan, and serious loss may then be a real possibility. If a satisfactory backup plan cannot be worked out, then it may be necessary to go to the additional expense to maintain redundant systems if the data processing need justifies it.

Programs and system independence

The need to transport programs from one system to another is a requirement if one desires to use a backup computer system. Much can be done to make programs as independent of a particular system as possible. Programs should be written such that they are not dependent on any specific piece of peripheral equipment. If possible, all programs should be written in a high level language such as Fortran or Cobol instead of a machine level language. Additionally, all manufacturer system software standards should be followed. Programs should be designed to use the smallest amount of main memory, within reason, for the task being performed. Some computer manufacturers provide information on compatibility between their various systems. This information should be taken advantage of if it is available.

Backup support facilities

Certain vital computer support facilities should not be overlooked in planning for use of a backup system. Even if a compatible backup computer system is available, lack of proper data preparation facilities may preclude its effective use. Availability of proper forms and other data media should be considered in the overall backup plan.

Check off list

1.
Is manual processing of data a practical alternative in times of computer system outage?

2.
Is the data processing function sufficiently critical to warrant the use of duplicate hardware?

3.
Has the use of backup electrical power and air conditioning sources been considered?

4.
Has the use of another company's computer been considered as a backup contingency procedure? If so, have program compatibility problems been evaluated?

5.
Have all critical computer system support functions been considered in the overall installation backup contingency planning?

OFF-SITE STORAGE OF EDP RECORDS

6

It should be anticipated that any disaster which might wreck computer hardware will also destroy data files, computer programs, and vital organization records. The need for data security continues, whether information is stored in steel filing cabinets, in a deck of punched cards, or on magnetic tape.

Figures compiled throughout the United States over a number of years indicate that about half the companies that lose the bulk of their records go out of business. This does not necessarily mean, of course, that the loss of records is the sole cause of failure. If flood, hurricane, or fire has wreaked havoc, the firm has usually sustained other losses besides records. Floods can engulf a company and obliterate an entire business section. Fires and explosions can raze buildings, incinerate merchandise and equipment, and put key personnel out of action.

At the same time, it would be a misconception to think that once a company is deprived of records it cannot, given sufficient energy and capital, reestablish and rebuild itself. But it is apparent that if key business records have been protected against damage or loss, they can immeasurably lighten the difficulties of reconstruction following any type of disaster.

It is because of these considerations that business has long recognized the hazards inherent in a high concentration of vital records in one location. During World War II and in the years that followed, the problem of duplicate record storage was given considerable attention by institutions and business. In some instances this interest was spurred on by the possibility of atomic attack. Worked-out mines were converted to record storage vaults, and tunnels were bored into solid mountains of granite.

In one of the most elaborate programs of this type undertaken after World War II, the Du Pont company placed its important records in a fireproof,

The need

waterproof, and atomic bombproof vault. This installation was equipped with a solid slab, armor-plated door, a smoke detecting system, and an electric generating plant—all in a 71,000-cubic-foot vault. The idea was to provide a successor management in case of an atomic attack or major disaster that wiped out major facilities and some population centers. These stored records were regarded as sufficient to aid Du Pont officials in the resumption of business activities.

Undoubtedly, few companies can afford to plan an installation that would compare with the Du Pont vault. Further, with magnetic tapes and discs the need for such large storage areas is greatly reduced. But the relative ease with which EDP records can be destroyed emphasizes the need for management to consider the desirability of an off-site storage area for data. By concentrating on protection of only the most vital data, the expenditure of money and effort can be held to reasonable limits.

Duplicate storage of valuable records is somewhat similar to an insurance policy, a backup system by which a firm hopes never to collect. All of this is based, of course, on the idea that a disaster would never be so far-reaching as to destroy widely separated storage locations in the same incident.

The basic rule in computer file maintenance should be this: "The current version of a file should never be released for processing until it can be reconstructed."[1]

Some executives and EDP employees concentrate so intently on the possible consequences of destruction by militant groups that they ignore the more likely and, hence, perhaps even more serious risk of destruction by "acts of God"—fire, flood, hurricane, tornado—or by mere operator error.

Many catastrophes seem beyond the realm of possibility. This is why a great deal of apathy exists

---

[1] Robert V. Jacobson, "Providing Security Protection for Computer Files," *Best's Review*, May 1970, p. 42.

concerning the problem of making certain of the survival of a computer installation after a disaster. Good intentions for future action, however, will not compensate for the loss of effort, skill, and money that may be concentrated in the EDP system.

The possibilities for the destruction of on-line data fall into three general types of situations:

Destruction of on-line data

1. Destruction because of improper input;
2. Destruction because of a mechanical failure; or
3. Destruction because of a program error.

For example, improper instructions to a program or a program error may cause the destruction of a data file. Malfunctioning tape or disc drives can render tapes and discs unusable.

It should be noted that perhaps the only real protection against such on-line destruction is the capability for reconstructing files from machine readable data media, stored off-line from the computer.

To cite an actual case, consider the example of the bank in a small Texas city:

The bank recorded its daily records on discs and duplicated this information on another set of discs. Each day the previous backup disc was destroyed. A program error on one set of discs made it necessary to use the backup system, and a machine error caused the destruction of the backup system. As a result, the bank was forced into a costly program to reconstruct its records— a disaster some institutions could not weather.[2]

If records are in constant use and the quantity is large, exact duplication may not be the practical answer. Duplication of the updated records could prove to be both time consuming and extremely expensive.

Backup systems

In many instances a three-generation backup

2 Carl B. Johnson, "Protection Primer For EDP Records," *Banking*, December 1969, p. 85. Reprinted with Special Permission from *Banking*, Journal of the American Bankers Association. Copyright 1959 by the American Bankers Association.

system is cheaper to maintain and is more practical. This involves storage at a separate location of earlier versions of the file, together with the transactions needed to reconstruct the current version.

This is also known as the "son-father-grandfather" method. It works as follows: the "son," or up-to-date file, is a combination of the "father," or previous file, plus the transactions necessary for updating. The run prior to the "father" is called the "grandfather" and is frequently maintained at an off-site storage location. On a rotating or cyclical basis, the "great-grandfather" file is destroyed, leaving the three-generation backup protection. This system affords considerable security, especially if the earliest version is stored in a protected area at a distance from the computer.

It may be noted that off-site storage may be maintained on a mixed data media if equipment allows. In many instances it would be too expensive to maintain a complete backup system on discs, but the disc operated system could be backed up on tape stored data at reasonable cost.

Some firms even go to the trouble to maintain a five-generation backup system, with off-site storage of at least one generation and a transaction history.

Record evaluation   Cost is a realistic delimiter in the preparation of backup copies of computer data. The choice of an acceptable method must be based on variables peculiar to the individual business, such as the number of files, the type of storage media, the frequency of updating, the available storage space, and the amount of funds available. An exceptional data protection plan will be wasted if its cost serves to paralyze other features of the data processing system. In most instances, extensive protection for a one-shot program would represent needless loss.

Before establishing the firm's duplicate files, management must make basic decisions which will determine the way the file system is organized. In the first place, a method must be set up for deciding which are the essential records. A balance must be struck between the desire to copy a large number of records and the cost of duplicate storage media.

Some companies have arrived at an evaluation of truly vital records as making up only 1 percent to 2 percent of the total data on hand. Other firms have found that the percentage of essential files must be considerably greater. But duplication of records, simply because it would be nice to have them on hand, is usually too costly and too difficult to implement.

What constitutes a vital record? It is hardly possible to generalize. A basic record for one firm is not necessarily an essential record for another company in a different type of business. Obviously, if a firm is to overcome a physical catastrophe that wipes out a substantial part of its plant, it must have a file which includes some detailed information about its facilities and products.

A practical classification can be made if management considers an individual record as being either vital or not vital. There is no middle ground, no comparable degrees of essentiality. The fact that a record is "useful" or "important" is not enough. The value to be placed on an individual record should be based on what the record can accomplish for the firm.

As a possible side benefit from this record analysis by management, some company officials have advised that they had never previously realized the extent of information available in company files.

Frederick Lutter has identified vital information to be retained in a well-secured area inside the general EDP area, and also separately as backup off site, as of two general types:

1. Master files in magnetic form controlled by serial number with release dates.
2. Programs and other software in primary language, and, where advisable, in the secondary or object language version—with all the program documentation and runbooks that are available. This physical program protection must be policed periodically. Source

programs in primary language should not be accessible to operating personnel. If in card format, they should be maintained in the programming area.[3]

Off-site location

The off-site storage location does not necessarily need to be separated from the EDP area by a great physical distance. The location should be sufficiently remote that it does not become involved in any potential disaster at the primary location.

Preparation, transportation, and storage of these files all represent points of vulnerability for theft, copying, or an off-line printout. There is no question that possession of a reel of tape provides an interloper a chance to examine the data at his convenience.

Some firms go so far as to deliver duplicate tapes by armored car guards. At the other extreme is the hardware store in Minnesota that prepares a monthly duplicate of the accounts receivable file and mails the tape to the home address of one of the firm's key executives. Other methods have been worked out by security minded institutions and companies.

If the remote storage idea is followed to a logical conclusion, however, the off-site location should be something more secure than the glove compartment of the comptroller's automobile. And, here again, the establishment of a proper environment for storage means more physical security. A combination controlled, fireproof vault may be ideal in most instances. If the requirements of security are critical, then a fireproof data safe should be used inside the vault.

The objections that are voiced by most data processing managers to the use of the data safe at the remote location fall into three classes:

1. The relatively high initial cost,
2. The problem of operating inconvenience, and

[3] Frederick H. Lutter, "Keeping the Computer Secure," *Administrative Management*, October, 1970, p. 10. Reprinted from *Administrative Management*, © Geyer-McAllister Publications, Inc.

3. The restrictions of security that require the vault always to be closed.

But it is something of a logical impossibility to put a price tag on the protection of EDP records which a firm must have to do business. Almost any reasonable cost in effort or money may be less than the value of the records it pays for.

Of course, one way to cut cost is for companies to pool their duplicate records to achieve protection. Group action can spread the expense, but the confidential nature of an individual company's records must be preserved. Unless there are adequate controls to limit access to authorized officials, the duplicate records may be in jeopardy.

Turnover is necessary at the off-site location, as at any record storage area. As a generation of tape becomes obsolete, it must be replaced. Almost all computer officials understand the need to maintain completely updated duplicates of all important program and data files. It is in the enforcement of this basic security measure that some EDP personnel become lax. Here again, this may be traceable to the pressures of production.

Duplicate storage maintenance

After essential company files have been classified, it is comparatively easy to set up a routine for duplication and storage. The real problem is to maintain these controls, without exception. Unless there is verification by management of auditing personnel, the duplication procedures may turn out to be nothing but a "paper plan."

It is also suggested that backup records be maintained in the custody of an employee who is independent of those persons who have access to the primary tapes or discs. This will insure that the backup materials will not be available, in the event an employee with access to tapes or discs suffers a mental breakdown or determines to sabotage the original materials.

Security

A reliable system for maintaining and verifying off-site storage should include the following:

Summary

1. That duplicated files are those which are essential,
2. That the duplicates should be maintained at an off-site location at such a distance that it would not be harmed by a disaster at the primary location,
3. That off-site storage is always made on schedule at a secure place, and
4. That an independent person has custody of the backup materials.

In general, there is no shortage of ability in the EDP community to furnish adequate protection to computer based information systems as soon as management provides the necessary supervision, planning, and resources for the off-site location.

Check off list

1.
Has off-site storage of data been considered as part of EDP operating procedures?

2.
Is off-site storage of EDP data financially feasible?

3.
Has reconstruction of EDP data been included in disaster planning for the installation?

4.
Have criteria to separate essential records from non-essential records been established?

5.
Is separation of duties among primary site and off-site personnel strictly enforced?

6.
Is the off-site storage procedure monitored to determine its effectiveness?

7.
Is the off-site location sufficient to avoid destruction by elements which could destroy the primary site?

ACCESS TO THE COMPUTER AND HOW IT IS CONTROLLED

7

"In order to destroy a computer, it is first necessary to gain access to it. . . ."[1]

Physical access to the computer installation should be restricted to only those individuals actually involved in the support of computer operations. Success in managing a secure installation is possible only through consistent adherence to this principle.

But it is just as essential that access be further restricted as to who can enter the computer room (machine room) proper. Most programmers, for example, have no business in the computer room unless they are working under supervision. As we will note in another chapter, a programmer with uncontrolled usage of the processor (computer) has the capability to initiate fraudulent schemes of several kinds.

To maintain good access controls, both to the building and to the computer room proper, it is usually necessary to place responsibility for security on the staff supervisor for each shift.

A striking example as to how loss may be minimized by keeping intruders out involved the bombing of the computer center of the University of Kansas, allegedly by student militants, in 1970. According to information released by university officials, doors were consistently locked after several bomb threats were received. Thereafter, only those individuals with a legitimate need were allowed inside the computer room. Subsequently, a bomb exploded against the outside of the machine room, blowing a six-foot-square hole through the computer room wall and causing damage to other partitions and walls throughout the structure. By preventing access to the interior, university officials

How access controls prevent loss

[1] "The Technology of Computer Destruction," *Broadside —Free Press*, 1970. (This is an underground newspaper.)

Illustration 12.
Placement of bomb
outside computer
building, University of
Kansas, Lawrence,
December 11, 1970

Illustration 13.
Bomb damage inside
computer installation,
from outside explosion,
University of Kansas,
December 11, 1970

were of the opinion that loss had been greatly reduced. Photographs of the placement of the bomb outside the building and interior damage appear in Illustrations 12 and 13.

Earl W. Wearstler, writing in *Banking,* recommends that "access should be limited to one or possibly two controlled points, depending on the number of employees and configuration of the computer facility itself."[2]

Unneeded doors may be simply bricked up. But in limiting access, it should be kept in mind that some fire exits may be necessary in order to comply with local fire safety regulations. Fire exit doors should be locked against entry from the outside, but instantly openable from the inside by pushing against a crash bar.

It is in keeping with good security to place audible alarms on all fire emergency exits. Alarms of this kind make considerable noise to alert supervision to the unauthorized opening, and they may be connected to a central guard station, if one is utilized. Alarms of this type continue to sound until deactivated by a key that should be controlled by supervision. A crash-bar alarm of this kind is seen in Illustration 14.

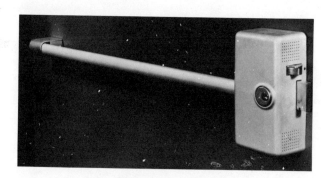

Illustration 14.
A crash-bar door alarm

[2] Earl W. Wearstler, "A Computer Center Is for Safety, Not for Show," *Banking,* April 1971, p. 70. Reprinted with Special Permission from *Banking,* Journal of the American Bankers Association. Copyright 1971 by the American Bankers Association.

Some businessmen state that they do not need control over access to the computer room, as "we have only a handful of employees. The presence of a stranger would be immediately apparent." While this statement is true, it should be emphasized that merely noting the presence of an intruder may not be enough. Restricting access is the basic requirement of security. Serious damage may have been done by the time an unauthorized person is first observed. Besides, in installations with few employees there may be times when no one is actually present to observe whether a stranger enters the premises.

In a larger system, maintaining control of personnel may present some added problems. The installation may be divided into several areas, each with individual security classifications. Some employees may be permitted in some areas, while restricted from others.

Then too, time is of the essence in almost any business, and it is usually desirable to grant entry with a minimum of delay. A number of electronic and mechanical devices are on the market that will control and facilitate entry. Of course, a lock and a simple door buzzer on the outside of the entryway can be used. This is sometimes known to security representatives and computer employees as the "badge and buzzer" technique. The employee who responds to the buzzer allows admittance on visual recognition or on the basis of a company badge. Of course, the employee granting admittance may be working at reduced efficiency, owing to the frequency of interruptions by the buzzer.

There are a number of mechanical devices that will allow entry without actually verifying the identity of the individual coming into the premises. A good lock, for instance, may furnish adequate security to the computer room, if keys can always be controlled. The problems here are that keys may be lost, keys may be issued to employees with no real need, and that keys may be duplicated without the knowledge of the keyholder.

Controls for small and large installations

Devices that allow entry without checking identity

In a recent security survey at the computer room of a Baltimore bank, it was noted that the keyholder hid the computer room door key in a hall bookcase. This was done so that the first employee reporting for work would be able to enter without waiting for the supervisor to arrive. Although no misuse had apparently been made of it, the hiding place of the key was known to a number of unauthorized persons.

Unless keying is done selectively, it will frequently be found that the EDP area doors can be opened by master keys, keys issued to all janitorial personnel, and stationary engineering personnel.

In a recent case in Ohio, a 19-year-old youth with a criminal record declined to explain why he was prowling a computer area. This youth had duplicated a key to the computer room without the knowledge or consent of his mother, a trusted employee in the tape library.

There are systems by which management may be able to determine which specific key was used to make an entry into a restricted area. A time lock system makes use of a printed tape that issues a written record inside the door lock unit. When the tape in this unit is removed, a printed record reflects the date and time of each entry, as well as an alphabet letter assigned to each outstanding key. While this type of control has some valuable security applications, it is "after the fact" security. Such a system merely records entry after it was accomplished by anyone who managed to obtain a key.

The combination push-button lock

An access control device used at computer centers with some frequency is the combination push-button lock, operated mechanically or in conjunction with an electric door strike. Only those persons who push the buttons in the proper combination order can open the door. Thousands of combinations are possible on most of these locks. Therefore, when an employee severs his job connection, a new combination can be set in a minute or two to prevent continued access. Some locks of this kind will ring an

Illustration 15.
Combination
push-button access
control locks

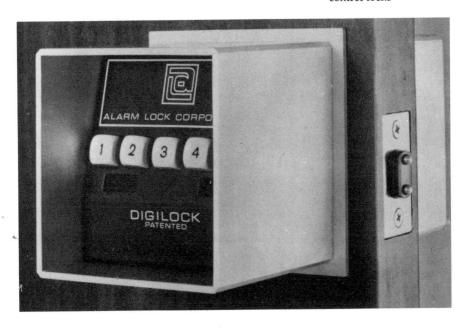

alarm when an incorrect combination is punched, alerting supervision to the fact that someone is tampering with the lock, or that the combination cannot be recalled. A system of this kind, of course, eliminates the need to keep an employee on duty at the door leading to the computer room. Two examples of this kind of lock appear in Illustration 15.

The card key system

Another access system which has been used for computer applications is the so-called "card key" system. This method makes use of a magnetically coded card which is inserted into an identification and locking unit. The front side of this card may be used as a company badge or identification card, with photograph, signature, description, and other vital information incorporated into the makeup of the card. An example of this type of access system appears in Illustration 16.

Illustration 16.
A card key lock

The rear surface of the card used in card key systems is commonly impregnated with ferric oxide, which produces a durable matrix suitable for magnetic digital recordings. The coding that is placed on this matrix allows only this card, or one similarly prepared, to open the door. The back of the card, however, is much like the tape on an average tape recorder, and can be erased with a magnet.

Instead of making use of magnetic coding, some card key systems make use of copper discs laminated into the plastic. This latter type is not secure against card copying. The nonmagnetic coding of this copper disc card prevents unauthorized identification of the code bit locations that are found on the magnetic type of cards; and the copper disc arrangement is not destroyed by running a magnet over the surface of the card. On the other hand, the location of the copper discs may be determined by placing this type of card under an X ray, or by disassembling the card for the same purpose.

A combination push-button lock may be used in conjunction with a card key system. This will combine the basic protective features of both. Knowledge of the push-button combination, as well as possession of a sensitized card would be required to gain entry. A thief who stole the necessary card could not gain entry, neither could an individual who learned the combination by peeking over the shoulder of a person in possession of the combination.

A combination of access systems

The coded key system, as seen in Illustration 17, makes use of a binary coded key and a solid-state reprogrammable logic control panel. The key codes in this type of system cannot be detected, even by X ray. An alarm circuit can be attached to sound an alarm should a ruled-out key be used, or should anyone tamper with the keyway. Millions of possible key combinations are available, and changes may be quickly made. The key pictured in Illustration 17 is coded through the twenty bits, or fingers, that comprise the circuit. By employing the total binary capacity of the twenty bits, a great number of combinations are made available. A lost or stolen key may be rendered inoperable immediately, but a factory coded replacement is needed to restore the system to a full complement of keys.

The coded key system

Illustration 17.
A coded key system

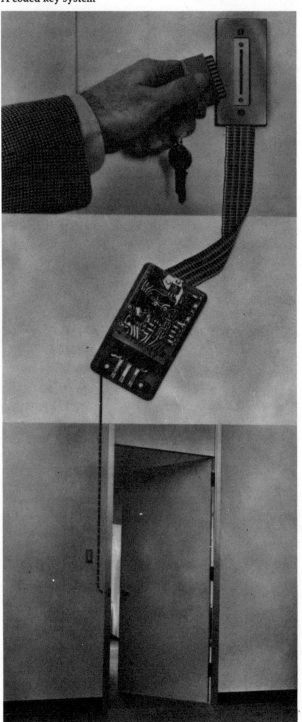

Only this key

tells this unit

to open this door

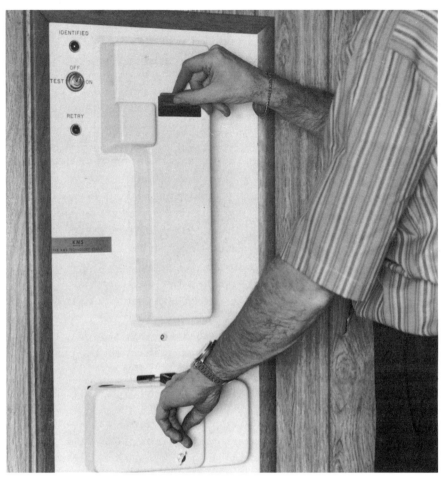

Illustration 18.
Automatic personnel or
fingerprint verifier

The fingerprint verifier

Another device which grants access to a restricted area is the automatic personnel verifier. This wall-mounted device contains a small film clip which is actually an encoded version of the bearer's fingerprint. A variation of this device allows the fingerprint to be mounted in an identification card that fits into the machine.

Access is obtained by simply placing the index finger into an input slot on the unit, and entry is granted in about five seconds.

Uniformed guards or CCTV

In some computer installations it may be desirable to restrict access by maintaining uniformed guards at the entryway. In some other locations it may be preferable to utilize a closed-circuit television system to view persons desiring access to the area. Along with a two-way communications system, a closed-circuit television (CCTV) will enable the guard to maintain control over a person who has not been issued a key, or who may have forgotten the combination to an electric push-button lock.

In another type of system, the employee must place his identification card on a badge reader and then look into the TV camera that covers the entrance. A guard or other employee inside the computer center can then make a visual identification of the person desiring entry as being identical with the person in the badge photograph.

Recording identity of the person granted entry

It may not be necessary to record the entry of each person granted entry into a computer installation. However, in some large data processing installations this may be very desirable. Some of the devices that are on the market make use of a computer type control console that receives information at the various entry gates from devices termed "remote readers." If this data corresponds with data already programmed into the system, then the closed door, gate, or turnstyle will be released. Cards that were issued to discharged employees can be blocked out, and this system serves as a means to check overtime.

When it comes to a choice as to which access systems should be used, cost will sometimes be a factor. Employee acceptance, the need for rapidity of employee entry, the reliability of mechanical parts, the need for human supervision, and the physical capabilities of the equipment may all be considered.

There is no single control system that can always be regarded as infallible. Practically all systems have some weaknesses, or may be subject to the failings of the humans who utilize them. It is suggested that consideration be given to a number of these systems in deciding which may best serve the purposes of the installation.

With the introduction of new techniques and equipment, computer centers of all sizes have discovered that it is easy and inexpensive to maintain an effective employee identification system. For example, badges of different colors or coding systems enable a supervisor to tell at a glance whether an employee is authorized in a segregated keypunch area, computer room, programming library, or tape library. Supervisors or employees with authority to enter more than one area may be provided badges with multiple color backgrounds. If uniformed guards are utilized at the entrances to specific areas, guards may use the badge and its color markings to grant admittance.

Techniques that have been available for a number of years make it possible for a new employee to receive a permanent badge at the time he first goes on duty. In addition, badges incorporate easily recognizable, full-color photographs, virtually tamper-proof and inexpensive in cost. Prepared by an employee who has had only minimal instruction, these badges are practical because manufacturers have become systems oriented.

An employee identification number may be embossed on the badge in bar code language. Cards of this kind are, of course, compatible with data collection systems and computer codes. The badge

Choosing control systems

Badge systems

can be clipped to the employee's clothes, or suspended by a plastic backing inserted into a pocket. To gain entry to the facility, the card can be read when inserted into a scanner. This scanner in turn feeds information into the computer to identify the employee and to record the time of entry into the computer center.

Alarm systems

Unless the computer center is in operation 24 hours a day, 7 days a week, there will be times when sensitive areas are unattended by supervision. When a single employee is present, it is acknowledged that there is a greater opportunity for fraud. The unsupervised programmer may run programs of his own making, perpetrating an embezzlement and returning data to its original location immediately thereafter.

There are any number of alarm systems on the market, with varying degrees of reliability, effectiveness and cost. Alarms that function well in one application may be unworkable in another. Consequently, the advice of a reliable alarm company should be followed for each installation.

A metropolitan bank in a southeastern state goes to great pains to preserve physical separation between computer operators and programmers. These two kinds of employees enter the building through entrances on opposite sides of the building and utilize separate parking lots. An invisible light beam alarm system is located along the hallway between the computer operating rooms and the area assigned to the programming staff. A uniformed guard is regularly stationed in the hallway between the two areas. Even if the guard should leave his station, or respond to an emergency, an alarm would be sounded if one of the programmers or operators attempted to cross the hallway into a restricted area.

The security anteroom

In many installations it may be desirable to utilize a security anteroom, security vestibule, or "man trap" at the entrance to the computer room or the computer building. This room, large enough to accommodate one or two people at a time, utilizes

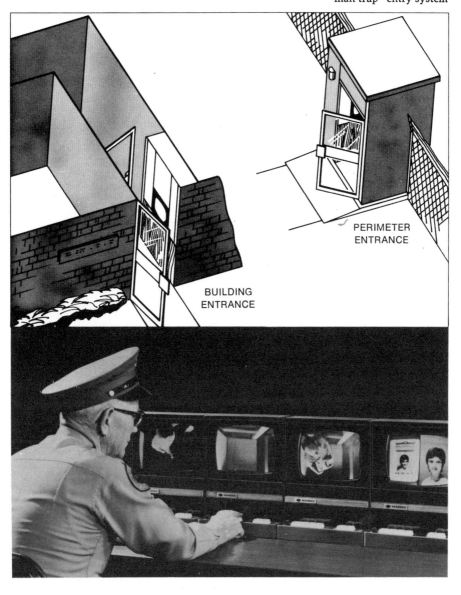

Illustration 19.
A security anteroom or
"man trap" entry system

PERIMETER
ENTRANCE

BUILDING
ENTRANCE

independently regulated doors at each end to regulate access. A good entrance control module of this type is that pictured in Illustration 19.

Deliveries

It is suggested that no packages of any kind be received in the computer center, except those for the computer engineer. It is preferable to use only employees or representatives of the hardware manufacturer for these deliveries. Unless regulations of this kind are in effect, it could be relatively easy to introduce an incendiary or explosive device into a vital area of the building through a messenger service.

Locking the hardware

Many computers operate 24 hours a day, and it could be pointless to place a lock on such equipment. Switch locks are available, if needed, to render equipment inoperable by cutting off electrical power. A switch of this kind would prevent an intruder from using a computer, even if he gained access to the computer room when it was unattended.

Check off list

1.
Is physical access to the computer installation actually restricted only to those individuals involved in support of the computer operation?

2.
Is access to the compter room further restricted only to those employees in operations?

3.
Are points of access limited only to those that can be controlled?

4.
Has the EDP manager considered use of: (a) a combination push-button lock; (b) a card key lock; (c) a combination push-button and card key lock; (d) a coded key system; (e) a fingerprint verifier; (f) a closed-circuit verification by armed or uniformed guards?

5.
Has consideration been given to a security anteroom or "man trap" for control of access?

6.

Has a badge system been installed for internal controls?

7.

Should an alarm system be used to further control access, especially when the computer operation has closed down?

8

THE ROLE OF SOFTWARE IN COMPUTER SYSTEM SECURITY

Computer system security is based on an interdependent triad of people, hardware, and software. All three factors are equally important. Failure of one of the three elements to be properly oriented to security can jeopardize the total system security.

A computer system is composed of hardware and software. Hardware is the actual physical computer. The computer hardware is composed of an interconnection of transistors, integrated circuits, resistors, capacitors, memory elements, and many other electronic and mechanical components. Software are sets of instructions which are stored in the hardware memory elements. These sets of instructions cause the hardware to perform actions that the programmer desires. For example, a program may cause the hardware to read data off a magnetic tape and produce a printed report from the line printer. In short, software or programs allow the programmer to make the hardware perform some desired design goal. To reduce confusion, it should be noted that the terms software and programs are interchangeable. Likewise, the terms hardware, machine, and computer are interchangeable.

In a real sense, a computer system is simply an extension of the person who programs it. That is, without a human to provide software (a program), the hardware will not perform. Thus results the computer system security triad of people, hardware, and software.

The importance of software security

The importance of software to the operation of a computer system is governed by the following direct relation—without software the computer hardware cannot function. Thus, minus software, a computer system has no productive value.

Even though software is not considered real property, its development and maintenance quite often represent an investment of thousands of both man- and computer-hours. Indeed, there are companies that value certain pieces of software in excess of $1 million.

The importance of software security lies in two areas: first, the necessity of software in making the computer system perform; second, the cost of software development and maintenance. A complete computer security system must not ignore the role of software.

The person concerned with computer security should be cognizant of the two major types of software used in computer systems. On the small-scale computer system, the development and upkeep of all software may well fall within the realm of a single group of employees. However, on a medium-to large-scale computer system the development and upkeep of software will usually fall upon two separate groups of employees. The first group is concerned with "operating system software." The second group is involved with "user software." These two areas of software should be considered in developing a total computer security system. In the sections that follow, these two different types of software and the types of security problems that they can present will be examined.

The two major types of software

The operating system software is a software system that provides common services to all user software. In a sense, it provides the person writing a piece of user software with a set of tools. For example, all user software performs input and output operations—for example, printing on the line printer, reading data from and writing data onto magnetic tapes, discs, etc. The operating system software provides input and output services to the user software. Thus, the person who writes user software need not be concerned with the minute details of making the hardware perform the desired operation. In this way, the operating system software performs a valuable function of relieving the person who writes user software of much tedious and repetitive work. Thus, the operating system software provides an environment for user software.

Operating system software

The services rendered by operating system software vary with the size of the computer system. In a small computer system the services provided by the operating system software are primarily concerned with providing input and output services to the user software. In a large computer system the operating system software provides many services in addition to input and output operations. Other services that may be supplied by the operating system include accounting for computer usage, identifying computer users, and maintaining data file storage. In computer systems designed for "simultaneous" use by more than one user—so-called "multiprogramming" systems—the operating system software is responsible for allocating available hardware resources among the users; in effect, it keeps the users out of each other's way. Commonly, operating system software is known simply as the "operating system." The computer hardware manufacturer normally supplies the operating system. The operating system software is often termed the "monitor" or the "monitor program."

As can be seen, operating systems have several functions that should be well understood in designing a total computer security system.

Security and the operating system

The security or lack of security of data stored on a computer system is greatly dependent on the operating system. This is because the operating system itself provides the mechanism for the storage and retrieval of data from devices such as magnetic tapes, discs, and drums. Two important points should be noted about data security and the operating system.

First, since the operating system is responsible for the storage and retrieval of data, it logically follows that the operating system can access any data stored on the computer system. This means that an individual familiar with the operating system and having access to or knowledge of certain identification codes can have a free hand with all data stored on the computer system. The difficulty of accessing all data on a computer system varies with each individual computer system. Ideally, the persons involved with maintaining the operating system should be the only people who possess the ability to access the computer system in an unlimited manner. More commonly, the computer system operator also has the information which allows unlimited access to data stored on the computer system. The information which provides for unlimited access to the computer system is usually in the form of a password supplied by the user to the operating system for identification purposes. The fact that certain personnel have access to these passwords and, thus, can access all data stored on the computer should be understood. The number of people having this unlimited access to data stored on the computer system should be controlled. Programmers writing user software have no reason to access data other than that concerned with their own projects.

The second point concerning data security and the operating system deals with computer systems that simply cannot offer protection to a user's data. This may be due to the lack of sophistication on the part of the hardware or the operating system or both. If this is the case with a computer system, sensitive data should not be permanently stored on the system itself, but should be stored in secure storage elsewhere. For example, magnetic tapes and removable magnetic discs may be removed from the computer system when the job is completed. In this way, the data will be protected.

The amount of protection given to data stored on a computer system is greatly dependent on the size of the system. Small computer systems usually provide little, if any, protection, simply due to the overhead and cost involved. Large systems with sophisticated hardware and operating systems can offer a great amount of protection against data access by unauthorized users. However, neither large nor small systems can offer protection from the person who has unlimited access to the data stored on the computer.

The operating system as an investment

By virtue of its role in a computer system, the operating system is a very critical item. Except in the smallest of computer systems, user software depends upon the services provided by the operating system. As a result of such a design, without the operating system, user software cannot function. Normally the operating system is supplied by the manufacturer to the customer as a set of what might be called "unedited" software. This practice is due to the fact that a manufacturer sells his hardware in many different configurations but usually writes only one operating system. The customer's or manufacturer's employees then tailor the unedited set of operating system software into a finished operating system for the hardware configuration at hand. This process is commonly known as "system generation." System generation often can require several hours of computer system time to accomplish. In both manpower and computer system time, generation of the operating system must be considered as an investment.

Backup protection of the operating system

Due to the critical nature of the operating system it should be protected by duplicate or backup copies. Normally, the size of the operating system is such that it is stored on magnetic tape for backup purposes. Copies of the operating system should be stored at secure locations in addition to being available at the computer system site. In addition, documentation pertaining to the particular version of the operating system being stored, along with any other peculiarities, should also be stored with the backup copies. If a situation arises that demands the use of a backup copy of the operating system, it may be essential to know exactly what version of the operating system is available. The updating of the backup copies of the operating system and its associated documentation should be a required duty of the personnel who maintain the operating system. It does little good to maintain a backup copy of the operating system if it is so out of date that it cannot provide needed services to user programs.

Destruction of the operating system, either by purposeful sabotage or by accident, can cause needless and expensive delay in computer system operations unless a proper backup scheme is employed. In dealing with situations where willful destruction of operating system software has occurred, it can be assumed that the malefactor possesses considerable knowledge about the computer system.

Recovery from the loss of the operating system by using a properly maintained backup copy is a relatively short process—usually a matter of minutes. When no backup copy of the operating system is available, the generation of a new operating system may take from hours to days. The actual time to generate an operating system is dependent upon the specific system and the time that is required to obtain the needed software from the manufacturer. It is preferable to maintain a proper backup copy if at all possible.

User software is software designed to make the computer accomplish a specific job such as accounting, payroll, billing, or other computer applicable tasks. User software (programs) can be manipulated for fraudulent ends. Manipulation of user programs is divided into two classes: first, the program itself can be altered; second, the input data to the program can be altered. Of course, manipulation can be deliberate or accidental. **User software**

Employee embezzlement represents a real danger in the use of computer accounting systems. Some publicity has been given to thefts of this kind, but this does not necessarily reflect the actual extent of the problem. Many firms shun any publicity that indicates employee criminality, declining to ask for prosecution of the offender. Some go so far as to hush up all reports of embezzlement, while other companies vigorously press for recovery from the bonding company but fail to furnish essential facts to the prosecutor's office.

Occasionally, the details in some of the more sensational cases are made public. For instance, between 1959 and 1963 the EDP manager of the New York stock brokerage firm of Carlisle and Jacqueline embezzled $81,120 by having checks made payable to imaginary payees. The accidental return of one of the uncashed checks brought the matter to the attention of the brokerage house.[1]

In another instance of this kind, a New York City antipoverty agency, the Human Resources Administration, was swindled of approximately $1.75 million during 1968. In this case the embezzlers processed checks payable to fictitious Youth Corps employees, reportedly at the rate of 102 checks per week. Through chance, a police officer found a number of the uncashed checks when investigating an illegally parked vehicle.[2]

Criminal manipulation of user programs

Program tampering is one way in which data processing systems can be manipulated for criminal goals. As an example, a program for the calculation of payroll checks could be modified to compute the salary of an individual in excess of what it should be. Normally, said individual is the one who modifies the program. Another ploy is to modify the payroll program to produce payroll checks for nonexistent employees. The checks are then collected and cashed by the person who motivated the plan.

An example of manipulation of a computer program for criminal purposes is provided by the case of an outside computer programmer for a Minneapolis, Minnesota bank who installed a "patch" on a computer program to prevent the reporting of his own bad checks. He then began to write checks without regard to his bank balance. This scheme was disclosed a short time later when the computer broke down and bank employees went back to

[1] *Wall Street Journal*, April 5, 1968, p. 1.
[2] *New York Times*, January 12, 1969, p. 1.

processing accounts by hand. This could have been extremely expensive to the bank, but the error was discovered after the overdrawn checks totaled $1,357.33.[3]

Achievement of criminal goals by program modification is attractive, due to the fact that the manipulation of the program's operation can be performed independent of the input data to the program. For example, payroll programs normally run by using an input file containing employee names, social security numbers, hours worked, salary range, and other information. Modification of the payroll program can produce bogus payroll checks without any alteration of input data to the payroll program. Modification of programs must be accomplished by someone competent in programming. When investigating a possible criminal manipulation of a computer system one should remember that a program can be modified to produce a desired action in addition to the normal function of the program. Also, if programs are stored on the computer instead of being stored on secure, removable storage, they may be susceptible to being modified without the knowledge of the people who normally utilize them for production purposes.

Criminal manipulation of input data

Criminal manipulation of computer systems can be performed by manipulation of the input data to user programs. In the example of the payroll program previously mentioned, data manipulation could take the form of modifying the input data to the payroll program, causing it to produce bogus payroll checks for nonexistent personnel.

Since the output produced by programs is a function of the input data, the security of data is of key importance to a computer system security program.

Designing a secure software system

Even though software is susceptible to tampering and manipulation, there is a great deal that can be done to provide for software system security.

Perhaps the most important single factor is an

[3] *Minneapolis Tribune,* October 13, 1966, p. 1.

overall data processing system design that is conducive to security. Most data processing systems consist of several programs, each performing a single task to accomplish the overall system goal. That is, in a typical business data processing system one would usually find separate programs for accounting, payroll, personnel, invoicing, inventory control, and manpower accounting. Also, many other programs are normally utilized to prepare the data for input to other programs. In a medium-sized business data processing system there might be in the neighborhood of 100 separate programs utilized. The relationships between these various programs greatly determine the level of software security found in the system. For example, bogus payroll checks can be detected by proper cancelled check processing. That is, comparison of the cancelled check with a data file of outstanding issued checks can determine its validity. Even so, there are businesses in which this verification is not performed and bogus payroll checks can be issued and cashed without detection. Additional verification for cancelled payroll checks might include a periodic audit against an active employee roster to establish the authenticity of the check's payee.

The goal of a secure data processing system design should be to minimize the likelihood of undetected, hence probably successful, criminal manipulation caused by alternation of a single element of that system—in short, attempt to force the person who would criminally manipulate a system to have to change several distinct elements in that system. In the payroll check example previously mentioned, proper cancelled check processing would force the person who desired to create false payroll checks not only to manipulate the payroll check program but to additionally falsify the active employee roster. Otherwise, the generation of false payroll checks would be detected.

Security at the program level

The design of each program that comprises the data processing system can contribute greatly to the detection of both intentional and unintentional errors associated with the input data to that program. Tests performed by the program for the correctness of input data are quite an obvious function to be included but are sometimes overlooked. These tests can be classified in two general categories: The first type of tests is concerned with the detection of accidental errors in the input data; the second type of tests is concerned with the detection of deliberate errors in the input data.

Detection of accidentally induced errors in input data should be a function included in all programs of a data processing system. This mainly includes detection of gross data preparation errors—for example, the inadvertent inclusion of alphabetic characters in a social security number. Incorrect input data may only result in an aborted or wasted program run on the computer. However, it is quite conceivable that incorrect input data can cause errors that will go undetected. These errors can propagate through the data processing system and cause inconvenience and financial loss. Indeed, the errors may never be discovered. For example, few customers will notify you of the fact that you did not bill them for the full amount of a sale.

Unfortunately, program detection of other than gross errors in the input data is difficult. The major burden for the development of error-free input data must of necessity fall upon the procedures used in the data preparation department. Some types of data are amenable to the use of a programming technique known as the "checksum." Commonly, the use of a checksum is also known as "batch totals" or "hash totals." A checksum is simply a total derived from some element of the input data. For example, if the input data was information used to produce checks to pay invoices, then a logical choice would be to obtain the checksum by summating the amounts to be paid. The computer program used to produce checks would independently produce a checksum and then compare its checksum with the checksum included in the input data. A discrepancy in the amounts payable would cause the two checksums to be different, thus indicating a potential error in the input data. The use of the checksum is subject to two limitations. First, an excessive amount of labor may be required to obtain a checksum when a large number of input records are present. Second, the fact that humans are prone to err makes it possible that a checksum discrepancy is due to a human error in the computation of the submitted checksum. When the quantity of data items over which the checksum is computed is not excessively great, then the checksum may indeed be a valuable technique. The checksum can also be used to verify the integrity of data produced by the computer. For example, the program used to produce payroll checks could produce a checksum over the amounts paid. The checksum could be used to verify that no checks had been removed prior to distribution of the entire batch of checks.

For certain critical data fields the use of a check digit can be justified. A check digit is simply a code produced from a data field and then appended to it. Whenever the data field is used, the program independently produces a check digit from the data field contents and compares it with the check digit appended to the data field. If the two check digits agree, then it is assumed that the data field is error free. Such a scheme can help to detect errors in the preparation and transmission of data to the computer. An example of a very simple check digit is that of casting-out-nines in arithmetic.

Additionally, programs should be designed to check information about input data files such as creation date, last date accessed, and volume label. This information is normally provided to user programs by the operating system and should be used to avoid using incorrect input data files.

Wasserman cites the mistake of a computer operator who erroneously used the previous day's master tape, which was retained as a backup. The computer program had been designed to recognize the error, and immediately printed out a message that the wrong tape had been mounted. But the operator ignored this information and pushed the restart button. The error was not discovered until 20 days later, and reconstructing the master file was very costly. A situation of this kind could have been prevented if the proper run number or version of the tape had been made a requirement for input.[4]

Development of a programming philosophy for the detection of deliberate errors in the input data should be based on the realization that many errors cannot be detected on the individual program level if the input data is altered in a sufficiently skillful manner. Such errors must be detected by the overall design of the data processing system. That is, auditing and checking functions must be designed into the data processing system. A program can be designed and written to validate functions requested

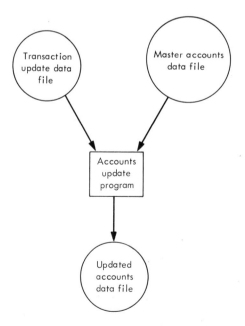

Illustration 20.
Data processing program with no input data to validate transactions

[4] J. J. Wasserman, "Plugging the Leaks in Computer Security," *Harvard Business Review*, September–October 1969, p. 119.

by the input data. To do so, however, requires the availability of validation information to the program which, in turn, can be utilized to establish the validity of input data. For example, Illustration 20 shows the flow of data in a program designed to update a data file that contains information pertaining to the status of various accounts in a business. Such a program could create and delete accounts on the master accounts data file, as well as provide for the posting of transactions. Thus, by including the proper input data, a fictitious account could be created and funds illegitimately transferred to that account. After the desired manipulations took place using the fictitious account, that account could be deleted using the same program. Without account validation information the program is not able to determine whether the request to create a new account is legitimate.

Illustration 21 shows the same program having an additional input of information pertaining to account validation. This information might include a list of authorized account identifiers and certain restrictions concerning the manipulation of the ac-

Illustration 21.
Data processing program
with transaction
validation data

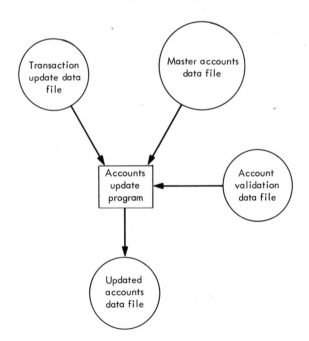

counts. This information might be included in the program itself. However, such a scheme forces the program to be changed whenever an account is to be added or deleted. More likely, the account validation information would exist as a data file. Thus, to create a new account, both the transaction update data file and the account validation data must be modified. If the account validation data is not available to be illegitimately modified, then the illegal account modification cannot take place.

In conclusion, the success of testing for deliberate input errors depends on the availability of validation data to individual programs. This data can be provided only if the overall data processing system is designed with security in mind. It is up to the system designer to develop a design philosophy which, as previously mentioned, will minimize the likelihood of successful undetected criminal manipulation of the data processing system through the alteration of any single element—program or data file—in the system.

Real-time computer systems vary greatly in design and application, ranging from airline reservation systems to management information systems. All real-time computer systems are designed to perform some task within a given period of time hence the name "real time." For example, an airline ticket agent must be able to confirm a passenger reservation within a matter of seconds in order to serve customers in a reasonable amount of time.

Security in real-time computer systems

Some system security control measures such as batch and hash totals may not be as effective in a real-time system as in a batch system. On most real-time systems data files are stored in on-line storage and are being constantly updated by transactions from remote terminals. However, a number of system security design measures are available to the real-time system designer.

Since incoming transactions are used to update files, all transactions should be saved until the updated files are backed up on off-line storage. Transactions may be saved on magnetic tape, disc, or hard copy, depending on the quantity of transactions that are being processed. A transaction record is valuable because of the insight that it provides into system operation. A transaction record may reveal irregularities of system operation that should be investigated.

All transaction programs should be designed to make as many checks on the validity of transactions as is feasible. The occurrence of detectable errors in transactions should be recorded and used as an operator and system control tool. The occurrence of a particular type of error among terminal operators may point to a system design deficiency. The occurrence of a high incidence of errors by a single operator may point to a training deficiency.

Additionally, all accesses to critical data bases should be tabulated by the transaction processing programs. In this way, a record of data base activity can be accumulated and used as a tool to spot deviations from standard system activity. All data base files should be printed out and audited on a surprise basis. Also, system data base files should be verified using data from outside the system, if possible. Of course, this is dependent upon the particular system and may not always be either possible or practical.

The real-time computer system designer may not have the flexibility of design that is usually found in a batch oriented EDP system. He should, however, strive to include all feasible validity and authentication checks. Also, he should include periodic quality control checks to insure that transactions are being processed correctly. Finally, he should design the system to collect transaction and data base activity information to help in detecting irregularities in system operation.

Dissemination of software information

Secrecy is a much-discussed word in today's society. However, secrecy can be important to a computer security program. Knowledge of the software used on a computer system is nothing more or less than knowledge about the entire data processing system and its operation. Infiltration into a security system is aided by such knowledge.

It would be foolish to attempt to have a data processing operation with complete secrecy. It simply is not feasible. However, programs and associated documentation should be controlled to the extent that they are available only to the personnel actually involved with their use and development. In cases where commercially available programs are utilized, the associated documentation often is publicly available from the vendor. Documentation concerning commercially available operating system software is also typically publicly available from the vendor. In such cases, any attempt at secrecy is futile.

Any software unique to the computer installation should preferably be controlled. This includes both user software developed for a particular task and any changes made to the operating system software.

Commercially available software systems to accomplish specific tasks are often utilized by data processing systems. These systems range from rather small programs available at small cost, to elaborate systems that are leased or purchased for large sums of money.

Protection of proprietary software

The vendors that supply such software systems often demand contractual guarantees that prohibit the dissemination of their software. The protection of such proprietary software should be included in any computer system security plan.

Check off list

1.
Is the role of software in security properly understood by management?

2.
Is the computer operating system properly backed up? Has documentation been prepared that explains how to use the backup copy of the operating system?

3.

Are the installation personnel who have access to all data stored on the computer known?

4.

Is the level of data security afforded by the computer system known to all personnel?

5.

Is there an overall design philosophy for the data processing system that attempts to provide detection for program and data manipulation?

6.

Do programs in the data processing system make all possible checks for incorrect input data?

PROCEDURAL CONTROL FOR THE COMPUTER SYSTEM 9

As noted in Chapter 8, computer system security is an interdependent triad of people, hardware, and software. The interaction of people with the data processing system is crucial to the overall effectiveness of a security system. The implementation of proper procedures can help to regulate the interaction of personnel and the computer system, thus improving the security of the system. Poorly implemented or nonexistent procedures can jeopardize the security of a computer system. However, some companies still feel that procedural controls can be ignored under the EDP environment, points out Joseph J. Wasserman in the *Harvard Business Review,* since the computer does not make mistakes. Mr. Wasserman notes, however, that "the computers don't make mistakes. But computers are programmed and operated by humans who still do make mistakes."[1]

Procedural controls involve systems which guide employees to work in accordance with management designated objectives. Some of these controls cost only the time for analysis and the vigilance of supervision.

If the mere posting of instructions and procedures would induce EDP employees to do what they are supposed to do, supervision would not be necessary. But the operations manager must take whatever action is indicated to close the gap between desired performance and actual employee work patterns. It is apparent, then, that the control system is no better than the performance of the people who run the EDP operation.

In practically all instances, it has been a breakdown of procedural controls that can be credited

[1] Joseph J. Wasserman, "Plugging the Leaks in Computer Security," *Harvard Business Review,* September–October 1969, p. 120.

with many of the mistakes that have plagued business and institutional computers.

No two organizations have identical requirements for computer security, neither do they have equal facilities for implementing their requirements. Consequently, there can be no hard and fast rules as to which procedural controls may be necessary. Procedural controls that regulate operations should be formulated after all system operations have been analyzed. It may be desirable to bear in mind throughout this analytical process that the chance of accidentally destroying, duplicating, or misprocessing transactions is always present.

Some of the procedures that may be put into practice involve nothing more than a rerun of the job being processed. In other situations, a highly complex system may be needed, utilizing programs designed especially for a specific type of failure.

Once again, it should be pointed out that the operating procedures adopted should evolve from a systematic analysis of the security needs of an individual situation. Compliance will be assured through continuing supervision and the adoption of protective measures. As circumstances change, a new analysis of security needs may be indicated.

Separation of duties

Under old, manual record systems, it was almost a ritual for employees to lock up the ledgers and journals at the close of the working day. Duties and responsibilities were carefully separated among employees. But under data processing, one employee may combine functions that were formerly assigned to several business units. In some instances, centralization of record keeping with the computer eliminates a number of the double checks under the old system.

With computer records, there are no erasures or other telltale marks, no adjusting entries. If an alteration is made, it is done cleanly, and the wrongdoer needs access for only a minute or two—perhaps even a few seconds may be sufficient. Meanwhile, the very complexity of the system makes misuse harder to detect.

Of course there is always a possibility that an employee in any system may succumb to temptation and alter records to embezzle money. This is far less likely if controls in the system require the collusion of two or more employees for the embezzlement to succeed.

Nevertheless, management in some EDP systems has ignored this fundamental separation of duties. This is often because of a scarcity of operating people with computer experience.

Some computer installations have strict rules prohibiting fraternization of programmers and operating employees. This nonfraternization applies to social as well as business contacts. In a large, impersonal institution or business this may be workable, but such a prohibition can present a number of problems in a small EDP installation.

Making separation of duties effective

A major eastern banking chain has effectively separated programmers and operators by requiring these two classifications of employees to enter widely separated entrance gates, to park in segregated lots, and to enter work areas through entrances on opposite sides of the building. Continuing this separation, cafeteria access, coffee breaks, and toilet facilities are provided in different areas of the building. Passing from one area to the other with a written pass is possible only during hours of controlled supervision. At other times, an alarm system and uniformed guards prevent traffic between programmer areas and operating areas.

Security guards should make certain that no one is allowed in the operating area, regardless of high position or title in the company, without signing a register showing access.

An actual case illustrates the loss that can occur through a failure to effectively separate employee duties. A vice president of a New York City stock brokerage company entered the operating area on weekends, without accounting to anyone. Because of his executive position and the fact that this official was in charge of computer activities for his firm, no one questioned his after-hours visits. During these clandestine visits the brokerage official altered input card decks that were scheduled for processing the following Monday. These alterations credited the official's personal brokerage account with a cash receipt and debited a large income account an equal amount to keep the books in balance. He also took the precaution of changing cards with control totals to include the fraudulent cards he had added. Then the wrongdoer prepared a credit memo to the margin department.

The brokerage official subsequently withdrew cash from his account. Eventually apprehended, this man had defrauded his employers of approximately $250,000 over a period of five years.

There were a number of things wrong here from a procedural standpoint, but the embezzlement would never have been possible if separation of duties had been enforced by general management.

As to other controls that were overlooked in making the brokerage house fraud possible, it was obvious that cash receipt forms were not numerically controlled and audited. Input data was not controlled under lock and key prior to processing. Also, there was no comparison between cash receipts deposited and cash credited to accounts by the computer. In addition, the company income statement was not audited, so that debits to the interest income account went undetected.

Three general types of procedures

Programming, operating, and testing and control comprise the three general types of computer system procedures. Programming procedures are concerned with the design and creation of new computer programs. Operating procedures deal with the daily production operations of the computer center. Testing and control procedures deal with testing the operation of programs for validity and accuracy and with controlling the usage of programs. Also, tests may be made to determine the level of security present in the system.

The writing of programs should be performed to meet the design goals specified by the EDP system design personnel. These personnel are responsible for originating an overall EDP system design that incorporates the required level of security. On the basis of the overall system design, specifications for the individual programs which make up the system are obtained. These specifications detail input/output data formats, required program operations, and other constraints on the program. Procedural controls on programming should provide for the following items:

Programming controls

1. The development of all programs should be documented according to a specified documentation standard. Information on documentation methods and standards is available from several sources.[2] Program documentation should progress in parallel with development of the program. This is to minimize the problems that can arise when it is necessary for other personnel to understand the program. Too often, programmers ignore documenting a program and give the reason that "I'm too busy writing another program." Lack of documentation can cause problems that are expensive in both time lost and money expended when it is necessary for personnel to understand the workings of an insufficiently documented program. This need can arise when a program must be changed or a newly discovered error corrected.

2. Personnel that write and develop programs according to prescribed specifications should develop these programs up to the point of acceptance testing of the program. At this stage, the

[2] Dick H. Brandon, *Management Standards for Data Processing* (New York: Van Nostrand Reinhold Co., 1963); M. Gray and K. R. London, *Documentation Standards* (Princeton: Brandon/Systems Press, 1969).

program and its associated documentation should be turned over to the personnel responsible for acceptance testing of new programs.

3. Personnel involved with the development of user programs for an EDP system have, for the most part, no reason ever to be in the computer room. Programming personnel should present programs to be run to the operations personnel. If a programmer has a legitimate reason to be present in the computer room during the running of his program, his presence should be supervised by operations personnel. Only in very rare instances is the development of a program facilitated by observing the computer run the program.

Operations controls

Procedures concerned with operations help to augment security by insuring separation of duties among employees and by regulating the interaction of personnel with the machine. Some of the operational areas that should be covered in procedural areas are as follows:

1. Behavior of operation personnel in the computer room should be covered by procedures. No eating, drinking, or smoking should be allowed in areas around computer equipment or magnetic tape and disc storage areas.

2. Procedures should cover the submission, running, and return of programs and data. All programs in the possession of the operations personnel should be controlled in a systematic manner such that at all times the status of each program is known. To illustrate what can occur when programs and data are not controlled properly, the claims manager in a Canadian government-sponsored medical aid program removed some keypunch cards and prepared false input. The substituted cards consisted of fraudulent claims for payment to an office that had been rented under a fictitious name. The scheme would never have been possible, except that there was no protection afforded to input data. Control-

ling the keypunch cards was all that was needed to prevent this fraud. In making security surveys of EDP installations, it will sometimes be observed that a company will go to great lengths to store a tape file in a secure vault. Yet at the same time employees will leave the source cards in a cardboard box on the floor where they are subject to tampering.

3. Procedures should cover the interaction of operations personnel with personnel involved in certain maintenance aspects of the computer.

Hardware maintenance personnel must enter the computer room to maintain and repair the computer and associated peripheral equipment. At times when hardware maintenance personnel are at work, operations personnel should insure that all on-line data is removed from the computer or protected from accidental destruction. Procedures should provide for proper communication and coordination between hardware maintenance personnel and operations personnel such that misunderstandings about the status of the machine will not result. An example of what can occur when no such procedures are provided is that of a large university where it was common practice to have weekly maintenance on the computer. These maintenance activities normally destroyed all on-line data stored on disc storage. As a result, the operations staff was supposed to back up all on-line data on off-line magnetic tape storage. Since no procedures existed to insure that this would be accomplished, it inevitably happened that the on-line data was destroyed by hardware maintenance activities. Such a loss was unnecessary and expensive.

Software maintenance personnel must enter the computer room to maintain and update the operating system software. These personnel are the only programming personnel that normally have any justification for being in the computer room and for operating the computer personally. For the most part, even these personnel do not need to be present in the computer room for most of their work. Here again, as in the hardware maintenance personnel case, procedures should exist to coordinate and communicate between the software maintenance personnel and the operations staff.

In the case of both hardware and operating system software maintenance personnel, one deals with highly trained specialists. Care must be exercised not to unduly restrict the activities of these personnel since inefficiency and lost time can be the result. However, procedures should provide for the supervision and coordination of their activities in the computer room.

4. The maintaining of an operation log should be covered by procedures. The operations individual who is in charge of the computer room should be responsible for maintaining a log that reflects the status of the computer at all times. Whenever the computer is turned over to hardware or software personnel, the log should be signed by all individuals concerned, and all activities should be detailed in the log.

Properly maintained, a log is valuable because it makes the operations personnel conscious of their responsibility of controlling the computer and provides a documented history of problems encountered in the computer operation. A log provides operations management personnel with the major source of information about equipment downtime and recurring problems, for the purpose of error analysis. All downtime and instances of machine halts should be included in the error analysis by management. A careful examination of this information can often be used to prevent the recurrence of minor problems before they become major. It is recommended that operations management maintain a permanent master file of known errors. If broken down into specific categories, by computer errors and operator errors, management may study the log to determine the source. Thereafter, corrective action can be taken. Error analysis may reveal, for example, that a specific operating employee is incompetent for his current job assignments, or that he needs instruction and guidance as to how data must be handled under security requirements.

In one case, an institution in California discovered that a defective magnetic tape drive had incorrectly processed a number of reels of tape. The faulty equipment was distorting data at random, but the source of the problem was not discovered for a considerable period of time. Had a continuing program of error analysis been in effect, it would have been noted that every reel in question had been processed on one specific magnetic tape drive. Suspicion would have been directed toward this piece of equipment and the source of the errors pinpointed at a considerably earlier date.

Additional error analysis information may be provided by the computer operating system. In many systems the occurrence of transient errors is automatically recorded in a data file in on-line storage where it can later be tabulated. Such information is invaluable for machine error analysis.

5. Operations procedures should cover the disposal of computer output and punch cards. Examination of discarded output can reveal much information about computer operations. It may be desirable to shred the material before disposal.

A salesman for a large computer hardware firm revealed the fact that it was easy to spot potential customers by looking for computer output and punch cards in garbage containers around industrial areas. A recent case cited by *Datamation* illustrates the extent of loss that may result because of improper or nonexistent disposal procedures. According to this account, Pacific Telephone Company incurred a loss of approximately $1 million due to theft of supplies. In this scheme, materials were ordered in an apparently legitimate manner, using the firm's computerized ordering system. Items that had been ordered were thereafter picked up by the thief at the regular delivery location. The excess orders were not noticed, since they were in excess of quantities picked up by employees in the usual operation of the business. This swindle was made possible because the thief gained detailed knowledge of the firm's ordering and operating systems from material taken from company trash containers. Included in this material in the trash were ordering system instructions, manuals, data, and computer program listings.[3] There seems to be little reason to bother protecting data and computer output if the results are put untouched into a garbage container to be seen by anyone who desires to lift the lid.

Operations procedures

When formulating operations procedures, it should be remembered that the operations personnel interact with the computer and perform much of their work in the computer room. Procedures should be designed not to hinder the operations staff but to provide for orderly operations that can be supervised. The operations staff should be made aware of what personnel have need to access the computer and what supervision should be provided for such personnel.

It is recommended that operations personnel provide supervision of all programmer activity in the computer room. The operations log should reflect all programs and data used. If possible, all user programmer activity in the computer room should be kept to a minimum and be subject to supervisory approval.

Procedures for highly confidential operations

In some cases it is desirable to consider certain data or programs as being highly confidential or secret. This classification should not be indiscriminately applied, since, if properly done, it will incur expense and time.

All highly confidential data and programs should be stored off-line on removable discs, tapes, or cards, except when actually being used. Such data should never be stored on-line on the computer.

[3] "News In Perspective," *Datamation*, February 1973, pp. 121–22.

The storage area should be highly secure for such items.

When processing such programs and data, all personnel except those authorized to deal with the highly confidential data should be required to leave the computer room. All remote terminals should be electronically disconnected from the computer. All scratch tapes and discs used with the job must also be considered as confidential material. Additionally, any output devices that use an impact printing method—line printer, Teletype—must have their printing ribbon removed at the end of the job and stored with the programs and data in secure storage.

All programs, data, and output associated with a highly confidential operation should be plainly marked "confidential" or "secret."

At the end of processing a highly confidential job, all of the computer main memory should be cleared by a program or hardware procedure. Additionally, procedures should be developed to provide for the disposal of no longer needed output, punched cards, tapes, and discs associated with highly confidential information. This would include shredding paper output and punched cards. Data on magnetic tape can be destroyed by writing long records of meaningless, random data on the tape. It is recommended that this be done three times with different record lengths so as to completely overwrite all original data areas on the tape. Similar operations can be conducted for magnetic discs. When a tape or disc that contains highly confidential data is found defective, it is advisable to physically destroy it.

Adopting highly confidential processing procedures is expensive and time consuming. A definite need for such a level of secrecy must first be justified before engaging in such operations.

Testing and control is a function vital to the continued successful operation and integrity of an EDP system. Testing and control includes both auditing and quality control checks on the operation of the

Testing controls

EDP system. The testing and control personnel effectively act as an internal security group to check for irregularities and deviations from established procedures in the operation of the EDP system. The testing and control personnel should be independent of the EDP line management and must have sufficient technical competence to be able to monitor the EDP system operation. If sufficient resources are not available to set up such a group, then it is recommended that the EDP system be tested at unannounced intervals by an outside consultant with sufficient expertise to determine the integrity of the system. Some of the functions that should be covered by testing and control procedures are as follows:

1. Testing and control personnel should have procedures for the exhaustive acceptance testing of new programs and EDP system changes. Using trial data, they should verify that all design cases of the program function properly before releasing the program to the operational user for use on actual data. Without proper verification of program operation, data can be destroyed or incorrect results obtained with a corresponding loss of time and money.

2. Accounting of computer time usage should be a function of the testing and control staff. Accounting records provided by the computer should be tabulated and examined for irregularities. The amount of computer time used by each user should be correlated to the task performed by that user. The tabulation of computer time usage can also help to make management aware of the level of computer usage.

In spite of the need for management concern in this area, several cases of computer time theft have recently come to light. In some instances this misuse has reached the point where computer operators were, in effect, running a private computer service utilizing their own firm's equipment. Perhaps the ultimate in this kind of misuse was reported in 1971, when one business was forced to upgrade the company computer to meet a sharply increased workload. A case of this kind that received considerable publicity was that of the Chicago, Illinois, Board of Education, in December 1967. In this instance it was charged that the board's computer employees were operating their own processing firm. This type of activity may be more widespread than is generally supposed, since instances are reported with some regularity.

3. Checks and audits of data and programs is an important function that should be included in testing and control procedures. Programs can be checked by comparing the copy in use with the original copy which should be in the possession of the testing and control personnel. Such checks conducted on a surprise basis help to discourage program changes. Preferably, the testing and control group maintains the original source version of the program, releasing only the binary or machine language version to the user after acceptance testing is completed. Checks and audits of data files should be made for irregularities and verified with data from outside of the EDP system, if possible. If audit trails are utilized in the EDP system, these should also be checked. Periodically, on a surprise basis, input data to programs should be audited to discourage input data fraud schemes.

Security can be checked by introducing phony transactions into the EDP system to see if the system design can detect them. Additional checks on the system can be performed by randomly selecting a small number of transactions to be audited.

On real-time systems the testing and control personnel can utilize computer-collected information to monitor data file accesses, remote terminal activity, and the number and type of transactions performed.

4. Testing and control procedures should cover methods for needed program changes. Requests for program changes—either to correct errors or for operational reasons—should go through testing and

control personnel to the personnel in charge of the overall system design. Such a procedure should provide a permanent record of why a program change was initiated, who originated it, and who approved it. The procedure should provide for the updating of all program documentation and notification of all users affected by the program change.

Conclusion

Procedures are crucial to the proper running of a secure EDP system. They should provide for separation of duties among employees so as to force a successful fraud to be the work of two or more employees instead of just one individual. Procedures should provide for the orderly and regular operation of the EDP system. A relatively crisis-free EDP system is easier to keep secure than one in which crises or irregular situations occur regularly. Procedures should not be so complex and cumbersome that they will be ignored. Rather, they should attempt to define to each employee his role in the total EDP operation.

Procedures that deal with security, such as programmer access to the computer, should never be relaxed because of a crisis or training situation. There is little rationale in setting up procedures only to ignore them when they are needed.

The need for written instructions

As soon as procedures are formulated, they should be reduced to writing. It is recommended that these written regulations be reviewed regularly, to determine if:

1. Instructions are current,
2. Instructions are complete, and
3. Instructions are so clearly stated that they are subject to only one interpretation.

Security protection requirements should be defined to all operators by job function and responsibility. It is suggested that a signed copy of these requirements be retained in each employee's personnel file. If instructions are clearly stated and supervision insists they be consistently followed, many situations that could lead to loss will be automatically eliminated.

In a specific example of failure to utilize written controls, an inexperienced operator at a large New England manufacturing firm was not made aware of operating procedures. This operator bypassed a safety device in order to speed up the updating of a customer file. Because of his incorrectly learned routine, the inexperienced operator lost two thirds of each of two copies of the file. Fortunately, the company maintained a three-generation tape file on this data; and through an accidental change in work schedules, the third run of the file was by an experienced operator, who discovered the errors in time to prevent loss of the data. The monetary cost in this instance could have been staggering.

Of course, this case also emphasizes the need for careful supervision of inexperienced operators. Owing to rapid expansion in the EDP field, a continuing shortage of skilled computer personnel can be anticipated, with frequent turnovers and the hiring of marginal workers needing supervision.

1.   **Check off list**

Has an effort been made to provide for separate duties among computer system personnel?

2.

Have the employees been provided with written instructions describing the actions expected of them in the performance of their duties?

3.

Does the programming staff have a documentation standard? If so, do they use it?

4.

Does the operations staff have thorough procedures to follow concerning activities in the computer room?

5.

Are newly developed programs exhaustively tested before they are used in regular operations of the EDP system?

6.

Are EDP system procedures subject to constant review for effectiveness?

7.

Are EDP system procedures so complex and involved that they are simply ignored by the personnel?

SECURITY AND
REMOTE TERMINAL ACCESS

10

The use of remote terminals to provide access to a central computer site is found in many different business data processing systems. A time-sharing system which provides access to a general purpose computer for a number of remote users is a typical example of remote terminal access. An airline reservation system is a usage of remote terminal computer access for a very specialized function.

Regardless of the particular system, all remote terminal computer systems consist of three elements —the central computer system, the communication facility, and the remote terminal. Illustration 22 shows the interconnection of a remote terminal access system. The complexity and actual components that comprise each of these three elements depends, of course, on the particular computer system and its application. In general purpose time-sharing systems often the remote terminal is a Teletype and the communication facility is a dial-up telephone line. In specialized remote terminal systems the remote terminal may be hardware designed for specialized operator interaction such as a point-of-sale remote terminal designed to replace a cash register in retail sales. Additionally, so-called "intelligent terminals," which normally are comprised of a CRT data display/input unit and a small computer, are commonly used to format, edit, and store data for later transmission to the central computer. Remote terminals for the transmission of batch jobs to the central computer are common and may include peripheral devices such as card readers, line printers, card punches, and even tape drives.

Communication facilities vary, depending on the system design and the remote terminal used. Dial-up or dedicated telephone lines are most commonly used. Private company lines can be used when they are available. In systems that have a large number of remote terminals, the communication facility may actually include a small computer to concentrate data generated by the remote terminals. Illustration 23 illustrates how such systems are commonly configured.

Consideration of remote terminal systems is not complete without mentioning that central computer sites may also be interconnected by communication facilities for the transmission of data. Such systems might best be termed "computer networks."

Illustration 22.
A remote access
computer system

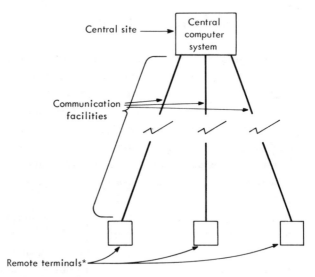

Central site → Central computer system

Communication facilities

Remote terminals*

NOTE: Number and type of remote terminals depends upon the computer design.

Vulnerability

News accounts during March 1971 described prosecutive action undertaken by the San Francisco, California, District Attorney's office against an employee of a Palo Alto, California, concern. Catching the fancy of the nation's press, this case was described by one West Coast newspaper as "computer rape." According to these sources, the loss was sustained by Information Systems Design, Inc., Oakland, California, which sells computer time and information by special codes through remote terminals. Allegedly, someone with the correct account number and identification had accessed the computer by telephone and had been fed data by printer hookup. But the victimized computer had been programmed to report any unauthorized access, and management of the computer was alerted.

After a search warrant was obtained, police allegedly found evidence in the Palo Alto office that connected the defendant with the stolen information. According to these sources, the stolen information was a computer graphics program valued at

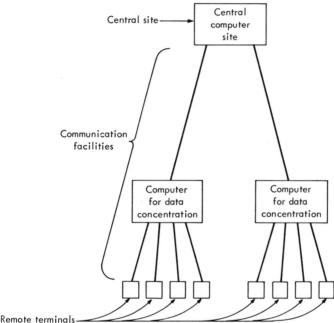

Illustration 23.
Remote access computer
system utilizing a small
computer in the
communication facility
to concentrate data

$15,000 to $25,000. One source stated that this type of unauthorized access had been going on for about a year. After criminal charges were lodged, a $6 million civil suit was filed against two employees of the Palo Alto firm. Recently, one of the defendants pleaded guilty to the criminal charges. He received a heavy fine and was placed on probation for three years.[1]

[1] *Los Angeles Times,* March 3, 1971, p. 1; *Wall Street Journal,* March 22, 1971, pp. 1, 17; "Telephone Used In Program Theft," *Business Automation,* April 1971, p. 7; "Crime of the Future," *Datamation,* January 1973, p. 122.

In a similar case, a teen-age youth obtained account and password numbers from a time-sharing computer system at Louisville, Kentucky. The young man had nearly worked out a program to bypass security safeguards when apprehended. He was reportedly extracting data from ledgers, as well as records of the computer firm's customers.[2]

In each of the above cases, an individual obtained access to the computer system by fulfilling the following three requirements:

1. Access to a remote terminal that was electronically compatible with the computer system communication facility was obtained. Thus the basis for access to the computer system was established.
2. The proper "credentials" or user identification was provided to the computer system, thus obtaining authorization to access the system.
3. The proper "language" or communication sequence was utilized in order to obtain the desired system response and thus consummate the fraud. Also, a knowledgeable user can obtain the desired system response by taking advantage of system weaknesses or loopholes, thus bypassing the normal communication sequence.

The above items represent the three security sensitive areas of remote terminal computer system operation. When system security is a concern, these areas should be examined and evaluated for their vulnerability.

Controlling access

The first requirement to be satisfied in communicating with the central computer is to have access to remote terminal hardware that is electronically compatible with the communication facility utilized in the system. Thus, the individual who desires to

[2] *Wall Street Journal*, March 22, 1971, pp. 1, 17; "Telephone Used In Program Theft," *Business Automation*, April 1971, p. 7.

defraud the computer system must first obtain use of remote terminal facilities. This can be done by either using the facilities normally used by the organization he wishes to defraud, or by using facilities from another source.

For example, in the case of a remote terminal computer system that uses dial-up telephone lines for a communication facility and Teletype machines for remote terminals, the individual could use a company Teletype if available. However, he could also rent a telephone line and Teletype to be used in conducting his criminal activities. Many common remote terminal devices such at Teletypes and CRT display/input devices are compatible and can be interchanged.

If all of the remote terminals are connected to the computer via "hardwired," dedicated communication lines, then the individual must have access to the system remote terminals unless he elects to engage in wiretapping.

Access to system remote terminals can be controlled by a number of means. Physical access to the terminal area should be controlled if possible. For even if other system safeguards thwart an individual who obtains access to a company remote terminal, much can be learned about system defenses by attempting to breach them. Another strategy would be to "lock" the terminal when not in use with a key type power switch. Needless to say, a knowledgeable user could bypass such a security measure and supply power to the terminal.

It is necessary to identify the remote terminal user in order to determine what computer system usage is authorized. Two basic means of determining user identification and authorization are available. These are as follows:

1. A password information exchange sequence between the computer system and the remote terminal user can be used to determine the identification of the user.

Identifying the user

2. A mechanical device can be used to read a user supplied identification badge or key to identify the user.

Password identification systems

Password identification systems usually require the user to supply an identification or account number and a password in response to questions sent to the remote terminal by the computer. The identification or account number is normally used for the accounting of computer usage. The password is used to verify the identification of the user. That is, if only authorized users have possession of the password. In this manner, unauthorized use of the computer system can be controlled.

Even though it is possible for all users to use the same password, it is more advisable that each user have a different password assigned. In this way, loss of one password does not jeopardize the entire password system.

Password user identification systems suffer from a number of inherent weaknesses. Passwords which should be committed to memory for secrecy may be written down by users not wishing to rely on their memories. Loss of the written materials can lead to compromise of the passwords. Users who feel they must commit their passwords to paper should carry such materials on their person. Additionally, the password should be written down with no other information on the paper. Such materials should never be left in desk drawers or left in the remote terminal room.

Theft of passwords can be accomplished by wiretapping or by the recovery of printing ribbons and platen impressions from hard-copy remote terminals. Also, passwords may be revealed by the hard-copy output of remote terminals.

Password user identification systems should be designed such that passwords can only be changed from one "privileged," physically secure terminal located at the central computer site. The user should never be allowed to change his own password. All user passwords should be changed regularly. Users who feel that their passwords may have been compromised should have their passwords changed immediately.

Passwords and account identification codes are normally stored on-line in a protected data file. The changing of passwords involves the updating of this file. The updating of user passwords should be a controlled operation that incorporates separation of duties among the personnel. The password file should be cross-checked by someone other than the individual who actually created the file. This is to prevent inclusion of unauthorized passwords and account identification numbers in the data file. The protection of the password and account identification number data file is crucial to the security of the password system because the information in the password data file is used to control access to the computer system.

Several variations on the password identification method are available. One scheme involves the use of a list of "one-time" passwords known to both the user and the system. Each time the user logs on the system, he uses the next password in the list. In this way, each password is only used one time. Thus a person who acquired a password from one remote terminal log-on could not use that same password to log on the system fraudulently. One difficulty encountered in this method is the dissemination of a list of passwords to each user and the protection of that same list from theft.

Another password scheme utilizes a mathematical transformation to provide a password response. For example, during the log-on sequence, the computer sends a random number to the remote terminal user. The user then performs a mathematical transformation on the number and sends the result to the computer system for verification. The computer system performs the same transformation and compares the user's result with its own. If the results match, the user is allowed to access the system. One such mathematical transformation that can be used is a pseudorandom number generator.[3] One problem with this method is that the mathematical transformation used may entail paperwork on the part of the user to obtain the answer and, hence, may lead to the discovery of the transformation by unauthorized personnel. Additionally, this method incurs extra work on the part of the user during the log-on sequence. However, if properly implemented, this system can make the theft of a single password useless.

Password discipline

In the password identification transaction between the remote terminal user and the computer system, several points of discipline should always be observed by the system. First, if a password identification sequence is initiated but not completed by the user within a given amount of time, the terminal should automatically be disconnected by the computer. Thirty seconds to one minute is a reasonable amount of time in which to respond to a log-on sequence.

The entire password and account identification number transaction should be completed before the information supplied by the user is verified. In this way, if the user supplies incorrect information, the system can respond with an "invalid information" message. Systems that respond with messages such as "invalid password" or "invalid account number" provide the prospective system intruder with information about the password identification sequence.

The remote terminal user should be given two opportunities to complete the log-on sequence correctly. After two incorrect tries, the remote terminal should be automatically disconnected. All unsuccessful log-on attempts should be recorded as to time, date, remote terminal, and password and account numbers supplied by the user who tried to

[3] Don E. Knuth, *The Art of Computer Programming*, Vol. II (Reading, Mass.: Addison-Wesley Publishing Co., 1969).

log on. Such a record can give insight into attempts to infiltrate the system.

Mechanical user identification systems make use of a user supplied badge or key to provide access to the system. Normally, in a password user identification system one need only know how to operate the remote terminal and supply the proper password in order to access the system. In a mechanical system the remote terminal is locked and inoperative unless the proper badge or key is inserted. Thus, whoever supplies the proper mechanical identification device is allowed system access. Mechanical identification systems reduce the time needed for log-on.

However, mechanical identification systems have some security weaknesses. If the necessary key or badge is left in the remote terminal by a forgetful user, it may be available to an unauthorized user. Additionally, mechanical identification devices may be stolen, duplicated, or manipulated so as to provide for system access by unauthorized personnel.

One mechanical device consists of a key and keyway which identify the user and control access through a logic board. This unit has the capacity to rule out selectively a particular user or group of users. It sets off an alarm in the event of tampering. Coupled with a printer, this system provides a printed record of the time, the specific user, and the location of the terminal through which entry was gained.

A combined password and mechanical user identification system can help to reduce the chance of unauthorized system access.

Once the identity of the user has been established by the system, it is necessary to determine what programs and data files are available to that user.

Determination of user authority can be accomplished in a number of ways. One common method is to utilize a user identification or account number that is composed of several parts. One method uses an account number made up of a department number and an employee number. Another scheme uses

Mechanical identification systems

Determining user authority

an employee number and a project code to make up the account identification number. When the user logs on, he is only allowed to access files and programs that are identified by his department number or project code.

Another scheme utilizes a table of authorizations based upon the user identification number. Whenever the user requests an action to be taken, the authorization table is inspected for approval.

In most large systems it is necessary to have provisions for various users to share programs and data files. This need should be considered in the system design or purchase. Normally, the ability to share files and programs is integrated with the system's method of determining user authorization. Often, this need for sharing goes beyond simple sharing of files and programs within a single department.

Sharing files and programs

In many large, remote terminal computer systems there is a need for users to share files and programs in a controlled manner. For example, user A may create a data file and desire that no other user except user B be allowed to access the file. Additionally, user A may desire that user B not be allowed to do anything other than read the data file. A user may require that a program is accessible for use by all users but that no one except himself is allowed to alter it. To fulfill these needs various means of control and protection of file and program usage have been developed.

Most of these methods are based upon designating one user as the "creator" or "owner" of the file or program. The owner of a file has authority to define the usage of the file by other users as well as the ability to manipulate the file in any way he desires. The owner grants usage to other users in the form of permissions to read the file, to add or write to the file, or both. Additionally, the owner can deny any usage of his file to users who have no need for access. The situation is similar for programs. The owner of a program can give permission to users to execute the program, to change the program, or both. The programs and data files that a user has need to access depends upon the type of transactions he is required to process. Each user should only be allowed to access the data files and programs that he requires to perform his task.

Additional protection of data files can be provided by the technique of "lockwords." A lockword is simply a password that must be supplied by a program when it desires to access a data file that is locked or protected by a password. Hence, in addition to needing the owner's permission to access a lockword protected file, a user's program must supply the correct lockword, or the access will not be allowed by the system.

The system should be designed to log all attempts to access data files that failed due to a lack of the proper permission or lockword. Such incidents may be accidental on the part of the user, but, on the other hand, repeated attempts to access protected files may represent the efforts of an unauthorized user attempting to infiltrate the system. One technique used to gain access to a lockword protected file is to write a program that is designed to attempt repeatedly to access the file, each time with a different lockword. Usually, the lockword is a short string of alphabetic and numeric characters. As a result, repeated tries with all possible combinations of lockword characters may allow for discovery of the lockword of a protected file. Such an attempt to discover the lockword would be noticed in the system's log of unsuccessful attempts to access files.

Logging unauthorized attempts to access files

Two other methods that may be used to bypass protected files both depend on system design weaknesses. First, some computer systems allow the user to examine the contents of main memory in case a serious error occurs in the user's program. This information is normally known as a "core dump." This is permissible if the user is only allowed to view areas of memory that are directly concerned with his program. However, some systems allow the user to examine the main memory used by the operating system. An intruder can take advantage of this data by attempting to access a protected file and then causing an error that will cause the system to divulge the contents of main memory. Enough information may be available to allow for the discovery of the lockword of the protected file plus other information that facilitates accessing the file. Any core dump facility should divulge only information pertaining to the user's program and absolutely nothing else. The second method of illegally accessing protected files is possible if the system allows the user program to utilize "interrupt-level" or "end-action" coding. The exact technical details are not important; suffice it to say that, given the proper end-action or interrupt-level coding privileges, a sufficiently competent individual can bypass all system protection and safeguard measures. In short, he is free to sabotage and steal throughout the system as he pleases. If a computer system permits end-action or interrupt-level coding that allows a user to sabotage the system, it is questionable to use such a system in a remote terminal environment. One computer utility company that utilized such a system simply could not keep files secure. A short program written by a malicious user was able to read all files on the system—even those files protected by lockwords. When leasing computer time from a remote terminal computer utility, it is important to understand exactly how much security is afforded by the design of the central computer system. System loopholes may make file protection an unattainable goal.

Wiretapping

In many cases it may be possible for a professional intruder or business spy to infiltrate a remote terminal computer system through the use of wiretaps. Virtually all remote terminal computer systems utilize leased public telephone lines for data communication purposes. Most known wiretaps have been located near the beginning of the leased line, because it is difficult for the intruder to identify the desired telephone wires once they have passed into the telephone trunk lines.

Remote terminal computer systems are vulnerable to wiretapping techniques. If an adversary is willing to go to the expense and trouble of wiretapping a remote terminal data communication line, chances are he has a good idea of what information or result he desires to obtain.

For example, if he desires to obtain a password in order to log-on the system at some later time, all he need do is listen on the line to the log-on sequence. If the wiretap allows him to enter data on the line, he may wait and utilize the system after the user has logged on, but while it is idle between transactions. Such an intrusion is commonly known as a "between-the-lines" entry. If the wiretap permits, the intruder may send "error" messages to the user's remote terminal asking that the user supply certain information in order to recover from the error. Such information may be the user's password or other critical information. However, just listening on the line can reveal almost all of the user's operation to the knowledgeable intruder.

Electromagnetic radiation from certain types of remote CRT terminals can also be detected and used for wiretap information. However, due to the fact that the radiation is of a very low level, there must be no interfering radiations from other equipment if this method of snooping is to succeed.

Two techniques are available to help guard against the use of passwords discovered by wiretapping. First, when the user signs off or logs off the system, he is required to supply the time that he expects to log-in again. Any attempt to log-in before that time would be treated as being unauthorized. Second, the use of one-time passwords or mathematical transformations, as previously mentioned, may thwart the use of passwords obtained by listening on a wiretap.

To help reduce the possibility of a successful

Defenses against the wiretap

139

between-the-lines entry into the system, the central computer should automatically log off any user whose terminal has been inactive over a certain period of time. The length of inactivity that will cause an automatic disconnect should be based on the type of transactions normally done at the terminal in question.

Several types of communication cable designed to thwart the application of wiretaps are available. A special type of cable made by the Mosler Safe Company is designed to set off an alarm at a guard room or control station if the circuit is disturbed by an attempt to apply a wiretap. This cable is suitable for direct burial, but the manufacturer states that it is practical only for relatively short runs within a facility or for limited distances between specific locations. When the circuits involve transmission through commercial lines, it would not be effective. The Mosler "security cable" utilizes a jamming signal on the outer conductor to protect the inner conductors.

Another type of security cable relies on an outer chamber of pressurized air which sets off an alarm if punctured. This type of cable is also operable for only short distances.

Cryptography

Cryptography is the art of writing in secret characters or ciphers to prevent unauthorized individuals from having access to the text. The history of cryptography is thousands of years long. Many varied schemes of encoding and decoding messages have been tried. Virtually all cryptographic schemes rely upon the use of a "key" to encode and decode messages. The key is either a string or table of characters, depending on the encoding method being used. Attempts to decode or decipher an unknown code usually hinge on discovering the particular key used to encode the message. The job of the person attemping to decode or "crack" an unknown code is facilitated by having a lengthy encoded message available for scrutiny and knowledge of the contents of the message. Normally, a person attempting to crack an unknown code has some idea of what type of information he is dealing with—that is, accounting information, personnel information, etc.

Many data encoding and decoding devices are available to provide real-time data encoding and decoding for transmission of data between remote terminals and the central computer site. Such a device is the Data Sequestor (trademark registered). This device encodes the text prior to transmission and decodes the text upon reception, according to a prearranged code. This code can be changed at will by the user and more than one-half million code sequences are available.

For transmission of data between computers, programs can be used to implement the encoding and decoding of data.

If cryptography is being considered as a means to secure data communications, the following items should be considered:

1. The key to a code must be kept highly confidential or else the security of the code is jeopardized. Both the sender and the receiver must possess the key. For maximum security, keys should be changed regularly.
2. Knowledge of the encoded text being sent facilitates decoding by outside parties. Formatting of text, headings, dates, names, or other known characteristics of the text may provide sufficient knowledge to discover the key and break the entire code.
3. A secure data line should always be active so that the start and stop of messages is not easily detected.
4. In implementing an encoded data transmission system, one should remember that the integrity of the system is only as good as the reliability of the personnel who operate the system and possess the keys to the code.
5. The encoding and decoding equipment must be physically secure. The key for the code is nor-

mally set by a number of switches on the device. Physical security is necessary to protect the key from discovery. Likewise, if programs are being used to encode and decode data, they should be protected from disclosure.

6. The costs of encoding and decoding should be considered before implementing such a system. One must include the cost of the encoding and decoding devices, the cost of physical security for these devices, plus the cost of operational needs such as the controlled distribution of code keys to authorized personnel.

In conclusion, cryptography, if properly controlled, can be an effective means to keep data communications secure. However, it is a method that can have the aforementioned shortcomings, and these should be considered when evaluating a specific application.

Assigning passwords   The assignment of passwords to users for log-on identification and for use as lockwords should not be a haphazard process. Too often, passwords are assigned in a predictable manner. The person assigning passwords is likely to assign "Smitha" to user Smith and "Xroger" to user Rogers. The situation degenerates if the user himself assigns his own password. A user is likely to use an easy-to-remember password that means something to him. For example, user Smith might like to use "Sue"—his wife's name—for an easy-to-remember password.

The person should draw randomly from a list of all possible combinations of characters that can comprise a system password or lockword. This procedure can easily be accomplished by use of a program. Such passwords are meaningless and can only coincidentally bear any relation to the user. Hence, it is more difficult to make a meaningful guess about the user's password. Likewise, a list of random combinations should be available for use as lockwords for data file protection.

Unlike most centrally located batch processing systems, remote terminal computer systems have potential security weaknesses in the areas of data transmission, user identification, and file protection. To be certain that sensitive data and programs are not lost, these security deficiencies should be taken into account when designing a remote terminal computer system.

Conclusion

1.
Are all points of remote terminal access to the central computer site known?

Check off list

2.
Are all remote terminals physically secure?

3.
Are user identification passwords changed at regular intervals? Is the user password file secure?

4.
Can data files and programs be shared among users in a controlled and secure manner?

5.
Has the threat of wiretapping been considered?

6.
Is the data being handled in the remote terminal computer system sufficiently sensitive to warrant the use of cryptographic methods?

7.
If leasing remote terminal computer time, has the potential of central computer site security failures been fully explored?

8.
Are remote terminal user identification passwords assigned in a random manner?

11

PERSONNEL SECURITY

Business officials sometimes point to efforts expended by management and security representatives in implementing physical controls, claiming that their firm has a very effective computer security program. These statements may be based on the utilization of up-to-date electronic alarm devices, closed-circuit television cameras, a disciplined guard force, and other factors. But regardless of the number of safeguards that may be installed, the basic security of an EDP installation is no better than the integrity of the employees who work there. Many of the problems of security may be "people problems." If employees either do not understand their responsibilities, or do not live up to obligations, the results may be serious. In any business there must be a basic reliance on the integrity of the employees.

The maintenance of security in a computer installation requires training for employees, both in operating procedures and protective measures. The object of this training is to make certain that each employee is aware of his vital part in installation protection and does not, owing to habit, become heedless of responsibility.

Three aims

Personnel security has three basic aims:

1. To recruit dependable and stable employees,
2. To insure that employees continue to be persons of integrity, and
3. To keep before these employees the knowledge that management relies on them, individually, to preserve the integrity of the computer installation.

Characteristics of EDP personnel

On the whole, it can be expected that employees and supervisors at computer centers will be idealistic, high-minded individuals. While generalizations do not always apply, it is sometimes pointed out that computer employees exhibit somewhat different characteristics from the traditional image of old-time accounting and auditing employees who maintained the records of a prior generation.

In the first place, some managers point out that EDP employees tend to be profession oriented, rather than employer oriented. Computer operators, programmers, systems design specialists, tape room librarians, and even EDP managers are all members of a new class in the business world. They have often had little contact with the traditional auditing and control procedures of business, and sometimes do not appreciate the necessity for these controls. Since computer employees do not understand this need for auditing, they sometimes indicate that control procedures are an unwarranted interference that can barely be tolerated.

Because of the continuing demand for qualified EDP employees, there may be a minimum of concern for job security among these individuals. This need for technically qualified employees may contribute to frequent job changes by programmers and operators. A survey of 500 firms by the Diebold Group, Inc., as reported in *Nation's Business* in May 1971, noted the loss of 15 percent or more of EDP personnel every year.[1]

While this percentage does not indicate that EDP employees should be labeled as "job hoppers," it does lead to the conclusion that in many instances they may not develop lasting loyalties toward a particular employer. This kind of deep-seated concern for the employer is, of course, a desirable attribute from the standpoint of company security.

Imprudent hiring

Undoubtedly, some computer loss problems in recent years may be related to imprudent hiring practices. These cases did not arise by accident, but rather as the result of factors that may have been predictable and controllable.

Because of personnel shortages, some firms have hired EDP employees "out of desperation," restrict-

[1] "Industry's Untold Multibillion-Dollar Story," *Nation's Business*, May 1971, p. 63.

ing employment inquiries to verifying the level of technical competence. Some of these lapses have occurred in firms that traditionally investigate all "new hires," even those employees who are not involved in handling sensitive data. As a result of this failure, some persons of doubtful background have worked themselves into positions of trust.

This does not mean that an individual with a questionable background cannot become an acceptable employee. In a high percentage of cases, however, a man is a product of his prior employment and associates. Statistics indicate that an employee will perform in the future, much as he has in the past.

In this connection it may be worth noting that business cannot completely ignore social obligations that may be due to the society which supports the business establishment. While no one should ever be deprived of his right to earn a living, neither should a business be compelled to place an individual in a highly sensitive position after that person has demonstrated that he may not be worthy of trust.

With present-day increases in work force numbers, the possibility of hiring an unstable or dishonest individual, or of discharging a person who is secretly disgruntled, is greater than at any time in business history. So in addition to examining prior experience, it may be desirable to analyze mental attitudes, to determine if the job candidate might be inclined toward the urgings of radical groups.

Company concern for a new worker is often directed toward job performance and the possibilities for eventual advancement. But if the firm's personnel representative will systematically check former employers, references, and co-workers, it will often be found that the potential employee does not have the basic stability to justify a job offer in the first place. An unexplained period of years or months on the employment application form may be an indication that the applicant has been regarded as unemployable, has spent time in prison or a mental institution. On occasion, these lapses or apparent inconsistencies can be explained away through direct interviews with the applicant.

On the other hand, some of these unresolved periods in the applicant's past may never be satisfactorily explained. In other cases it may be found that the man is not actually a criminal, but that he is unstable, owing to pressures from his financial, marital, or personal involvements.

There are, of course, many instances when an employee performs in irrational or unstable ways without harm to his employer. But on the other hand, the employee with unpredictable activity patterns may switch labels on computer tapes, sell discs or tapes to a business competitor, or sabotage the tape library because of a grudge. By declining to hire an applicant who lacks stability, it follows almost automatically that security vulnerability in the computer area will be reduced.

But the question of technical competence should not be overlooked in the desire to obtain employee stability. One observer has pointed out that "It is important to recognize that an inspired bungler can sometimes do more damage than a thief or vandal . . . he could erase a magnetic tape file containing several years' historical data."[2]

Once an individual is on the job, some firms take the attitude that they must continue with existing computer personnel, regardless of the problems. In some companies EDP functions have been combined when employees resigned, or as a means of cost savings. This tends to make the installation dependent on a small number of EDP employees who grew up with the firm's system and have a corner on operating knowledge and techniques. This reliance on a handful of employees sometimes causes man-

Problem employees

[2] Harvey S. Gellman, "Using the Computer to Steal," *Computers and Automation*, April 1971, p. 17. Reprinted with permission from *Computers and Automation*, April 1971, copyright 1971 by and published by Berkeley Enterprises, Inc., 815 Washington St., Newtonville, Mass. 02160.

agement to hesitate in the adoption or enforcement of regulations that are consistent with good security. But no employee, regardless of job responsibility or the level of competence, should be allowed to ignore or circumvent approved standards.

Analysts who have reviewed numerous cases of business dishonesty sometimes point out that most employees considered themselves honest at the time they joined the firm. In some instances the problems of computer security may be directly traceable, not to lack of policy, but to failure of policy enforcement. Management should trust employees, but should not ignore responsibility to verify controls that regulate access and use of computer facilities.

Employee awareness   Then there is another aspect to a successful computer security program—not only should management hire stable people, but these employees should be advised that management relies on them to preserve the integrity of the installation.

It is usually found that a number of outside individuals are involved in data processing, including maintenance technicians, auditors, hardware and software salesmen, engineers, and janitorial employees. It is essential that employees at the installation take the initiative in regulating and controlling the activities of outside individuals.

Many computer employees are, of course, knowledgeable as to their responsibilities. But in most EDP installations a definite program is to be recommended, guiding employees and emphasizing to each individual the importance of his role. Professional security consultants sometimes call this "security awareness." An approach of this kind, usually involving brief meetings with no more than five or six employees at a time, should be handled by an individual who is able to command respect—a member of management or the head of security. Most employees will accept high standards and abide by posted regulations if they understand what management seeks to achieve, and the methods that have been adopted. Employee suggestions for security should be solicited and carefully considered as one aspect of this program.

For its part, management should develop a keen sensitivity toward the objectives and desires of educated and technically specialized computer employees. Of course, computer employees should not be favored at the expense of others. But it may be beneficial to make responsible employees aware of the objectives of security, and how this may benefit them individually. It is basic to the program that all individuals involved be made continuously aware of their individual security responsibilities.

Management should recognize that employees may change from time to time. Until recent years, few people seemed to question whether an individual's problems had any connection with his work performance. It was taken for granted that the employee would leave his personal anxieties and private feelings at the employee entrance as he reported for work, and would pick them up again as he left at the end of the shift. Data collected in recent years seems to indicate that emotional pressures may cause employees to change. Unintentional work slowdowns, machine halts, errors, and other problems in computer work areas may be directly related to emotional attitudes and pressures on employees. Because of the cost of replacement and training for employees, it is often better to locate and extend help to an emotionally troubled employee before serious damage results.

Of course, it is not expected that management should be "his brother's keeper." But when it becomes obvious that an employee has severe emotional problems, counseling and help may be in order. It may be less expensive to show sympathy for marital and financial problems, and to help the employee obtain a needed personal loan, than to discover that he has sold a confidential computer tape or has decided to vent his frustrations on the computer installation. In instances of this kind, management may prevent a breakdown in character and

Employees with personal problems

**Termination
procedures**

the security of the EDP installation may be saved.

When a computer employee resigns or is discharged, the individual should be asked to immediately turn in all confidential or proprietary company material. This should include the company badge or identification.

It is also recommended that the departing employee be required to leave the premises at once. This procedure will eliminate the possibility of grudge action at the time of discharge.

Then too, there should be rules against allowing a former employee to "visit" the installation, unless a proper escort is provided.

Hiring techniques

The responsibility for hiring computer personnel is of considerable importance to other individuals at the EDP installation. Through this process new talent may be continually fed into the employee reservoir from which managers and supervisors are drawn. Continued success of the program is directly dependent upon the ability to recruit, train, and motivate competent people to their greatest potential.

But hiring of employees is seldom a completely predictable process. A recognized authority on personnel security, B. Ernest Gorrill, has pointed out that "at best, hiring is a gamble. A competent personnel representative should not insist on hiring only 'sure things,' but he is a fool if he bets on too many 'long shots.' The important purpose is to select 'winners' by playing the 'favorites.' "

Stability and dependability may well be the most important attributes desired in computer employees. If an individual has previously shown signs of instability, there may be reason to question whether he will be stable in the future. At the expense of repetition, it should be emphasized that past activity is the best indicator of satisfactory performance in the future.

It is usually a comparatively easy assessment to ascertain whether the applicant has the experience and educational requirements to equip him for the position. It is equally important, but usually more difficult, to accurately relate the applicant's past to his job potential. This is the area in which an evaluation of stability assumes considerable importance. It is here that the judgment and experience of the personnel representative comes into play, to determine whether sufficient background information has been developed to assess stability with reasonable accuracy.

A generation or two ago it was not unusual for an individual to live at one address or in one neighborhood for many years. Due to changed economic and social conditions, the modern-day applicant may have lived at a number of addresses in a comparatively short time.

Indications of instability

Frequent moves are often indicative of a number of problems. Experience indicates that this may be an area which warrants detailed inquiry by the interviewer.

Of course, the official conducting the interview should refrain from any physical act or verbal expression that could convey disapproval of the applicant's past activities or current feelings. If disapproval should become apparent to the applicant, then it is unlikely that he will be completely responsive to any questions regarding critical areas in his past.

It is suggested that EDP application forms should always provide sufficient space for a listing of prior addresses for the last ten years. Many application forms do not provide sufficient space, and pertinent information in this regard may never be developed by the interviewing official.

One of the most effective tests of employee stability is to examine how the job applicant handles his financial obligations. If he is able to make payments to creditors properly, does not contract for unnecessary debts, and avoids garnishments, collections, and bankruptcy, then it is likely that the job seeker has the requisite discipline.

Financial responsibility

A man who lives beyond his resources, or too close to the limit, may be subjected to pressures that affect judgment. Should an unanticipated need for more money arise, resulting from an accident or his wife becoming pregnant, then debt delinquency may be the result.

Marital obligations

Of course, a man who has been married more than once is not necessarily a security risk; but if the applicant has been divorced or separated, a number of factors should be examined. These include the number of dependents that the applicant is obligated to support, the causes for divorce or separation, the ages of the parties, and the applicant's attitudes toward his responsibilities. An examination of marital status may provide strong indications as to the applicant's overall stability.

Arrest record and driving record

Involvement in illegal activities or an unfavorable driving record may also be good indicators of lack of job stability needed in the computer room.

Some firms or institutions have an inflexible policy against hiring anyone who has ever been arrested, regardless of the circumstances. This, of course, may not always be fair to the applicant, and it may be desirable at least to obtain his version of the facts that led up to any arrest. If, however, police detention or arrest was an outgrowth of a student protest or civil rights movement, EDP management should take a hard look at the facts before hiring someone who might sympathize with saboteurs.

Further, stable people generally try to comply with criminal laws and driving regulations. There are exceptions, of course. But as a general proposition, an individual who consistently fails to conform to authority cannot be expected to abide by security rules designed to protect a computer installation.

Emergency hiring

Because of the tight labor market in the computer field, it may sometimes be necessary to put an applicant to work before background inquiries can be completed. This should, of course, be avoided if possible. In instances of this kind, it is suggested that a policy be utilized to place the new employee on probation until all inquiries are completed and evaluated.

1.   Check off list
Does management realize there must be a basic reliance on the integrity of EDP employees and that this obviates the need for careful employee selection?

2.
Is there a training program to make sure each employee understands his vital role in installation protection?

3.
Are employees being encouraged to be installation oriented, rather than profession oriented?

4.
Are EDP employees hired "out of desperation," or is there advance planning for computer needs?

5.
Is there too much reliance on technical qualifications at the expense of security?

6.
Does management insist on continuing with a problem employee?

7.
Is management alert to changes in employees? Is help extended to those who appear to be unstable?

8.
Are employees required to leave the premises immediately if they are terminated?

9.
Does management insist on hiring only stable employees?

10.
Does management assess applicant stability by checking past residences, employments, and references?

11.
Does management judge applicant stability by an

examination of financial responsibility? By marital responsibility? By avoidance of arrest problems? By driving record?

12.
When computer employees are hired in an emergency, are they on probation until all personnel inquiries are completed and evaluated?

SABOTAGE AND DATA THEFT

12

There is scientific agreement that "a permanent magnet of sufficient strength, applied to magnetic tape in the right manner, will erase or seriously degrade data recorded on that tape."[1]

In recent years, news accounts have described a number of incidents of deliberate or accidental erasure of data on computer tapes. Running a magnet over a tape scrambles the makeup of the thousands of recorded characters, and there is no method whereby this harm can be undone or repaired. Further, since the data on the stored media is not visible to the naked eye, there may be no indication that damage was done until an attempt is made to use the tape or disc. It is immaterial whether the loss in a case of this kind may have been caused by hate or by accident. An erasure that is completely unintended may be no less damaging.

One West Coast data processing manager lost his job when a group of Boy Scouts touring the computer center happened to have some magnets with them that erased some of the company's records stored on tapes.[2]

Another reported loss was allegedly caused by an engineer for a well-known computer firm who made some repairs on the hardware of a commercial credit company. As is common with some engineers and repairmen, this individual utilized a magnetized screwdriver to assist in manipulating and picking up small bolts and nuts. Unknowing, the engineer scrambled the records of about 80,000 customers of the credit company when the screwdriver was placed in direct contact with the disc pack on which the data were stored.

In another case, a major eastern bank reported

Data erasure by magnets

---

[1] W. D. Tiffany, "Are Computer Files Vulnerable To Magnets," *The Office*, September 1972, p. 51.

[2] *Wall Street Journal*, March 22, 1971, p. 1. This appears to be another example of the harm that may be done when tours are allowed in a computer installation.

Illustration 24.
Sabotage inside the
Dow Chemical Company
computer facility,
Midland, Michigan,
December 1969

Illustration 25.
Additional view of
sabotage inside
Dow Chemical Company
computer facility,
Midland, Michigan,
December 1969

serious and recurring errors in lists of depositors' account records and in the bank's own payroll lists. Considerable investigation led to the conclusion that erasures were being caused by a magnetic door opener at the entryway into the tape library. Nothing happened until a cart of tapes was pushed into direct contact with this piece of door hardware. The magnetic door opener then apparently scrambled some of the data on the side of the tape nearest the entryway.

Another incident reported by the press stated that data stored in a manufacturing company's memory drums had been wiped out by an employee who unknowingly hung his magnetic flashlight on the unit while cleaning the inside of the drum cabinet. According to this account, the firm had no backup information available on tape, either at an off-site storage location or in the computer library. Working under emergency conditions, the company was eventually able to reconstruct data from original sources. During the interval, most of the functions of the manufacturer, including the computer center, had been closed down for six days.

Perhaps the most widely publicized case of this kind involved the sabotage committed by radical members of the Students for a Democratic Society in breaking into the facilities of the Dow Chemical Company at Midland, Michigan, in 1969. More than 1,000 tapes were unusable after this militant attack. Dow officials said that there is every reason to believe the damage was caused by small magnets left with the tangled tapes on the floor.

Quite understandably, news stories of damage by magnets have caused genuine concern among persons responsible for computer security. There seems to be little question that serious loss has been caused by magnets in a number of these cases. On the other hand, other accounts of damage that have been circulated appear to be nothing more than unsubstantiated rumors. One of these false stories that was repeated for a time was to the effect that a delivery truck carrying a magnet along a public street had erased tapes inside a nearby computer center.

Then too, some advertising matter has also clouded the facts concerning the security loss potential of magnets. One firm selling magnetic detecting devices asserted that "a magnet the size of a quarter can destroy a library of up to 50,000 tape reels in minutes." It was apparently because of this kind of advertising that *Business Week* asserted that "security men thrive on the wages of fear."[3]

Because of the conflicting information, the Stanford Research Institute made, during 1972, detailed scientific tests of the harm that could be caused by magnets of different strengths, shapes, and sizes. The Stanford tests found that a number of factors could affect the possibilities for loss. To generalize, the scientists concluded "that tape libraries are not as vulnerable to magnetic sabotage as alleged. While vulnerability exists, we believe it has been exaggerated."[4]

The Stanford researchers also concluded that "even relatively small separations between magnets and recorded computer tapes are likely to provide significant protection from erasure."[5] What this meant was that the separation of even an inch or less would be sufficient to prevent loss in many cases. A magnet of great size and strength may be more apt to cause damage, but this possibility becomes unlikely with a separation of several inches. It was also concluded that placing tapes inside a steel filing cabinet (double walled) gave good protection against most magnets.

The results of the Stanford research experiments have proved of considerable value in planning computer security. It is quite apparent from this research that harm cannot result by waving a magnet,

[3] "Security Men Thrive On the Wages of Fear," *Business Week*, June 20, 1970, p. 114.
[4] W. D. Tiffany, "Are Computer Files Vulnerable To Magnets?" *The Office*, September 1972, p. 52.
[5] Ibid.

	Magnet	Approximate Magnetic Field (gauss)	
		At Pole Edges	At Stated Distance
1.	Flashlight magnet (5/8" x 1-1/2"; 16 ga.)	800	45 @ 1/2 inch
2.	Small dipole disc (1/4 oz) (1/2" dia. x 1/4")	800	15 @ 1/2 inch
3.	Small horseshoe (2 oz) (1-1/2" x 1" x 5/16")	1100	10 @ 1 inch
4.	Small rod (1/4 oz) (1/4" x 1-1/4")	800	290 @ 1/8 inch 45 @ 1/2 inch
5.	Rod (1-3/4 oz) (1/2" x 2")	850	390 @ 1/16 inch 90 @ 1/2 inch
6.	Ferrite ring (8 oz) (4" dia., x 3/8", 1-1/2" center hole)	1000	100 @ 3/8 inch 95 @ 1 inch
7.	Large U magnet (4 oz) (1" x 3/8" x 1")	2000	900 @ 1/8 inch 280 @ 1/2 inch
8.	Magnetron magnet (6 lb) (6-3/4" x 3-7/8", 1-1/2" air gap)	3000	1800 @ 1/8 inch 680 @ 1/2 inch 420 @ 3/4 inch

Illustration 26.
Magnetic fields (in air) of some small permanent magnets (a magnetic field of 400 to 500 gauss is generally sufficient to cause a computer to misread tape)

somewhat like a magician's wand, in the general direction of the tape library. And it is reassuring to know that the vulnerability may not be as great as some have claimed.

But on the other hand, some cases of computer tape damage have been reasonably substantiated. The fact remains that almost any magnet, large or small, can be dangerous if brought into direct contact with magnetized data.

It may also be worth noting that it is not necessary for a tape to be completely erased in order for it to be rendered useless. If there is destruction of a number of spots of data on a tape, or enough damage to change sufficiently the magnetization so that the tape transport is caused to have a "read error" at a number of places on the tape, then that may be enough to render the tape useless to the user program designed to use it.

From all the available facts, it is apparent that caution should still be exercised in keeping magnets out of the computer room; nor should the study be taken to mean that magnetic detecting devices are without value in a computer security system.

There are a number of magnetometers and magnetic searching devices on the market today. A number of these pieces of equipment were developed originally to assist the airlines in detecting hijackers carrying weapons on board an airplane.

Magnetic detecting devices

Utilized in a doorway opening, a magnetometer will sound an audible alarm if anyone carrying a ferrous (iron) magnet passes through the doorway leading into the computer room. These detectors are not restricted to ferrous magnets, but will sound the alarm if any piece of ferrous metal is carried through the detector. The director of one EDP installation wears a metal leg brace as a result of injuries sustained in military action while serving his country. If this official enters the computer room, the metal which he carries sounds the alarm.

One of the problems here is that all magnets are not made of ferrous metals, and that some magnets cannot therefore be detected by most of the detectors that are on the market.

It may be a difficult problem to make certain that a disgruntled former employee, armed with a magnet, is kept out of the tape library or computer room under all circumstances. Nevertheless, this is essential.

Regulating former employees

If an employee is given notice prior to discharge, it is recommended that he be physically restricted to an area where there is no sensitivity. Complete removal from the EDP installation altogether is preferable.

A few firms have adopted a so-called "buddy system," for all computer room work assignments, insisting that one employee never be alone in the computer room. This may be good in theory, but as a practical matter employees often tend to ignore requirements of this kind while concentrating on their work loads.

The degausser

Some EDP installations make use of a degausser[6] to erase magnetic tape for reuse. Utilizing this device, a disgruntled employee in a midwestern location took a number of tapes from the tape library without authority and completely erased the data thereon. This loss could have been prevented if library access controls had been effective. This case also points out the potential danger of the degausser. It seems obvious that this device should be carefully controlled, with no chance for misuse, either by accident or by design.

In spite of the known dangers in all magnetic materials, recent business periodicals and computer magazines still contain advertisements of bulletin boards and wall charts with magnetic attachments, for use in computer areas. These devices utilize colorful markings and indicators, held in place on wallboards by magnetism. They are described as "being helpful in flowcharting, block diagramming, Pert networks, and in charting business procedures and sales programs." While these devices are undoubtedly of business value, if properly controlled, they should be looked on with skepticism in the computer center.

And because of the possibility of damage from magnetized tools, it is recommended that all company maintenance and engineering personnel be individually briefed regarding this hazard. It is also suggested that the EDP manager or shift supervisor personally oversee all maintenance and repair projects in computer areas, insofar as possible.

Other types of sabotage

Banks and savings and loan sources have reported instances in which a disgruntled employee switched

[6] From Karl Gauss, German mathematician (1777–1855), noted for his investigations of magnetism.

labels on computer disc packs or tapes. A tape librarian at a Los Angeles area firm was given two weeks' notice prior to termination during 1971. This individual promptly removed all labels on about 500 reels of magnetic tape, costing the company a considerable amount of money to reidentify individual reels. In searching for a criminal charge that could be brought against this culprit, the prosecuting attorney advised that a theft charge could not be sustained, noting that no theft had occurred. Neither had the disgruntled employee made an unlawful entry or breaking. The only criminal offense that seemed to apply was the relatively minor charge of malicious mischief. Since no one had actually seen the employee remove the labels, even this charge was not filed.

It is also to be noted that most employees in a computer installation are aware that a loss of electrical power may spoil a considerable amount of stored data in a comparatively short time. In at least some instances, unhappy employees have caused unnecessary damage by cutting off electrical power when other employees were not in position to observe what occurred.

Another technique that has been used to cause disruption and downtime has been that of making a telephone bomb threat against the computer. One West Coast clothing manufacturer reported eight calls of this type during 1970. Of course, if access controls are rigidly enforced, explosive devices should not be allowed to enter the computer room.

In a recent New York case, management officials continued to operate the company computer after a number of employees went out on strike. After a time it became apparent to the strikers that they had not interrupted the basic functions of the company, owing in part to the fact that management still had the ability to operate the company computer. When the significance of this was realized, some of the striking employees broke into the computer room and destroyed some tapes and programs to make certain that all business activities came to a halt.

Tape or program theft

So long as there are persons who benefit from industrial espionage, there will be thefts of computer data. This problem may be less dramatic than that of computer sabotage, but it is a real security problem, nevertheless. "It is not unheard of for programmers to walk off their jobs with important files and systems, and within 30 days, a new company is born with a full assortment of programs."[7]

A magnetic tape, with tens of millions of characters of data, can be duplicated in a matter of minutes, and there is nothing to indicate that the material was copied. And as obvious as it may be, the contents of magnetic disc and drum storage are easily copied onto magnetic tape, and may be stolen in a few minutes.

During the summer of 1970, Encyclopaedia Britannica filed a lawsuit against three night-shift operators, claiming that these employees were in a conspiracy to copy nearly three million names and addresses from the firm's most valued customer list. It was also alleged that one of these three employees had walked out of the building with a tape in his briefcase, and had used an outside computer service bureau to copy the names and addresses onto another tape. Thereafter, the list was sold to a direct mail advertiser. Damages in the amount of $4 million were claimed, with $3 million said to be actual damages and $1 million as punitive damages.

In another situation, "a major university reported an incident in which a university employee with computer experience, who was not a member of the computer center staff, was able to steal data. He entered the computer center while a confidential file

[7] "New Threats and New Defenses," *Banking*, August 1970, p. 70. Reprinted with special permission from *Banking*, Journal of the American Bankers Association. Copyright 1970 by the American Bankers Association.

was sitting by a computer awaiting an operation, processed the file, copied the information, and walked out."[8]

Strikers at a major airline recently indicated that they would pay a large sum for the firm's payroll list. Apparently, the intention here was to visit non-striking employees at their homes to exert pressure on those individuals. After a short time, an undercover agent approached the union officials who had made the original offer, indicating that the undercover man could supply the needed list for the specified price. At that time the labor officials stated that they had already obtained the employee list from computer files. Details as to how this list was obtained was never revealed.

To protect against theft of the tape or disc itself, one firm has developed a label that can be permanently attached to the tape reel. If the reel in question should be carried past a magnetometer at the entryway to the computer area, a warning signal will be set off. This device, of course, does not prevent the possibility that the tape could be copied inside the computer room.

Other devices that are on the market incorporate locks into the tape reel case, preventing removal of the tape for processing unless the lock can be broken or opened.

1.
Do all members of supervision and all computer employees understand the danger of allowing any kind of magnet to come into contact with tapes or discs?

Check off list

2.
If the computer installation utilizes a degausser, is it maintained at a safe distance from the tapes and discs that are not to be erased for reuse?

---

[8] William S. Bates, "Security of Computer-Based Information Systems," *Datamation*, May 1970, p. 65. Reprinted with permission of *Datamation®*, copyright, Technical Publishing Co., Greenwich, CT, 06830, 1970.

3.

If an employee is given notice of termination, is he removed from computer areas, where he could sabotage tapes, files, etc.?

4.

Are controls over tapes or discs such that they could be copied without observation, or actually carried away from the premises?

THE MILITANTS AND
MAN-MADE DISASTER

13

The vice president in charge of advertising for a major banking chain in an eastern state recently said that escorted tours of this organization's new computer center had stimulated more public interest than any previous attraction in the firm's history.

This bank official pointed out that extensive newspaper and television commercials were used to acquaint the public with details of the new construction. Thereafter, regular tours were scheduled, and large numbers of people eventually observed the decor of the building and the late model computers under operating conditions.

As a part of this firm's advertising campaign, thousands of detailed floor maps were passed out, showing the specific location and arrangement of Electronic Data Processing units, operating areas, programming rooms, and the tape library.

But balanced against the advertising benefits that may have resulted from public display of the bank's computer was a great potential for harm from a security standpoint. Even while these public tours were being conducted and floor maps distributed, student activist groups in the neighborhood of the computer center were describing this institution as "a prime example of the establishment which should be destroyed!"

With the benefit of hindsight, one of the ranking officials of this firm subsequently described the public tours and advertising campaigns as "needlessly looking for trouble."

It is because of examples of this kind that *Business Week* recently pointed out that "many computer centers sit in glass 'showcase' vulnerability."[1]

Public knowledge of computer locations

Another observer noted, "This is the nerve center of the bank. . . . How many banks would let visitors wander through the vault or would conduct tours

[1] *Business Week,* June 20, 1970, p. 114.

so the public could inspect the safe-deposit box facilities?"[2]

To show what can happen with even a well-intended visitor, Allen cited the following:

A large insurance company in an eastern city recently gave a ladies' garden club a tour of its EDP facilities. The spinning tapes and blinking lights impressed one visitor so much that she felt she had to have a souvenir of the occasion. She later said, "I hope I didn't do any wrong. There were all those boxes of cards on the table, and I just reached into the lid of a box and took one." Perhaps this later caused a program to be rerun. A more likely possibility is that the card may not have been missed at all, and the center is still trying to correct the resulting confusion.[3]

Another authority on this subject pointed out:

The idea that the computer is the showcase of the company . . . is out of date.

If security is to be taken seriously the administrative manager must first of all control nonoperating traffic. He should—

Hide, rather than highlight, the exact location of the computer center.

Restrict rather than encourage the number of non-company visitors. . . .[4]

In spite of this advice, another observer noted that "if one walks through the financial center of most riot-prone urban areas, one can see numerous computers through large street level windows."[5] And a Connecticut firm announced as recently as 1971 that the company's new computer installation was to be housed in a glass-enclosed circular room.[6]

Banking magazine has suggested one step beyond

[2] "New Threats and New Defenses," *Banking*, August 1970, p. 70.

[3] Brandt Allen, "Danger Ahead! Safeguard Your Computer," *Harvard Business Review*, November–December 1968, p. 100.

[4] Frederick K. Lutter, "Keeping the Computer Secure," *Administrative Management*, October 1970, p. 10.

[5] Harold Weiss, "The Danger of Total Corporate Amnesia," *Financial Executive*, June 1969, p. 64.

[6] "Housing Computers: How Four Firms Programmed the Job," *Administrative Management*, February 1971, pp. 34–35.

concealment of the location of the computer, recommending that banking institutions "keep utilities such as heat, water, power, and air conditioning away from public view as much as possible."[7] Loss of utilities could, of course, result in inability to use the computer.

It is not the purpose of this section to trace the historical or social development of the so-called militants. It may be somewhat incongruous for some of these revolutionary groups to refer to themselves as "student" militants. Needless to point out, however, many of these organizations have used the campus as a place to recruit volatile dissenters and those who are unwilling to wait for gradual social change.

Some of these militants have made no secret of the fact that they consider Electronic Data Processing installations as prime targets to be eliminated. This may be because the computer's concentration of vital information in a small area makes possible the total destruction of institutional or corporate records by fire, vandalism, or explosion. Then too, the computer is the symbol of the sophistication and automation of "the establishment."

Much of the destructive activity of the militants has been directed toward university or college computer installations, apparently with the idea that educational institutions could be forced to conform to their demands. But it would be a mistake to feel that universities and colleges are the only targets of these radicals.

During 1969, five members of an antiwar group calling themselves "Beaver 55" broke into the Dow Chemical Corporation's data research computer center at Midland, Michigan. Trained by the Students for a Democratic Society (SDS) in methods of destruction, these militants ransacked the center, scattering tapes and cards all over the floor. At first it appeared that the damage could be corrected with

[7] "New Threats," *Banking*, August 1970, p. 70.

reasonable cost, but cleanup employees found a magnet in the debris. No larger than a quarter, a number of circular magnets left by the members of "Beaver 55" had erased the data on approximately 1,000 reels of magnetic tape. The total cost to reconstruct the data was about $100,000.

A photograph of the tangled mass of printouts, tape, and punched cards at the Dow Chemical installation appears in Illustration 27.

Militants as technologists

It is no secret that the militants are well informed as to methods that may be used to destroy a major center of learning. Numerous printed reports have repeatedly pointed out that the way to wreck a university is to "get" the computer center.

But it is the underground, militant press that has printed specific details as to how this destruction may be accomplished. An article called "The Technology of Computer Destruction," is only one of several that have circulated through the underground press. Distributed through the Broadside—Free Press of Chicago, this article was allegedly printed in Canada by an anonymous member of the anticomputer culture. This article included the following instructions on how to wreck a computer:

To obtain access to the computer system: A list of relevant ideas might include breaking and entering, picking locks, bribing guards, infiltrating the data processing industry and pulling inside jobs, wearing gloves and masks, and leaving the scene quickly without bothering to call a press conference.

To harm the processor: The actual computer is best attacked through its wiring. The things to do to a couple of square yards of two-inch-deep wires challenge the imagination. . . . The guts of any computer are its electronic circuits . . . mounted on hard plastic cards that plug into the racks. The cards pull out of the racks . . . can be destroyed by cracking them in half; one might also consider ripping them off.

To harm magnetic tape: To destroy a reel of magnetic tape, one simply spools the tape out onto the floor and makes sure that it gets well kinked . . . the best way to wipe a tape is to bring it close to a strong magnet (or vice versa).

Illustration 27.
Scrambled tapes,
punched cards, and
printouts at Dow
Chemical Company,
Midland, Michigan

To harm magnetic discs: The disc itself can be destroyed by scoring the surfaces with a knife or a screwdriver. The read/write heads found on disc units and on tape drives are expensive and can be destroyed by rasping the surface with the tiny slits in it with a file . . . the fastest way to blow a disc unit is to open the door while the thing's spinning.

To injure punched cards: If the cards are bent, ripped, or even seriously frayed at the edges, they cannot go through the card processing equipment. . . . An interesting form of minor sabotage is to punch extra holes in every data card you come across. . . . The results may be surprising and pleasing. Many people doing that can really ———— up the system. . . . Punch cards to mail in (bills, etc.) can be most efficiently altered by a friend who has access to a "keypunch," because the sabotage is invisible, and often because it can be more sophisticated. Like changing the amount of a "debit" (bill) to a negative ("credit"). There's a story about a guy paid with punch card paychecks who altered the date on one January check to the previous year and blew up (that's a technical term) two years' bookkeeping.[8]

An attack with warning

On February 11, 1969, a Control Data Corporation 3300 computer was destroyed at Sir George Williams University in Montreal, Canada. A news account, describing this activity was as follows:

MONTREAL (AP)—Riot police evicted protesting students from Sir George Williams University and arrested about 80 last night, but the students wrecked the $1.6 million computer center. . . .

A ten-hour battle between the police and about 200 students ended the student occupation of the ninth-floor computer center that began January 29. The students were protesting the makeup of a faculty committee. . . .

The police were called in after the students began ransacking the cafeteria and turning on water hoses in the new $26 million Henry F. Hall building. . . . They destroyed both the university's computers with axes and set fire to the center.

When police and firemen arrived, they were pelted with pieces of furniture, computer tapes, and electrical parts, university records, registration cards, transcripts, and typewriters. . . .

[8] "The Technology of Computer Destruction." Broadside—Free Press, 1970.

The firemen managed to put out the blaze, but (the) university information officer . . . said smoke and water damage made the computer a total wreck.

Additional press accounts stated that about 2,000 students milled around outside the computer building behind a police cordon, creating disturbances and shouting encouragement to the students inside the building. In the meantime, some members of the crowd supported the police and firemen with shouts of "Go cops! Go!" Fighting developed among partisans in the crowd when militant groups from McGill University and the University of Montreal arrived to give support to the occupiers.

With the benefit of hindsight, an official of Sir George Williams University pointed out that some ten days elapsed between the beginning of the occupation and the beginning of destructive acts in the computer center. Undoubtedly the delay by officials may have contributed to the final result. A decision for prompt eviction might have prevented the personal injury and the destructive loss of property.

There was a considerable buildup of militant activity prior to the destruction of the computer center at Sir George Williams University. But there was no prior warning when three gasoline bombs were thrown into the computer installation at Fresno State College (California) on May 19, 1970. As one eyewitness put it:

An attack without warning

As I was going from the keypunch room through the operations control room, I heard shattering glass in the operations center, about 35 feet from me. As I entered the operations center, the mainframe was engulfed in flames and smoke billowed from the back of the machine. I could see holes in two windows behind the mainframe itself. I closed the doors to the operations center and hollered for everyone to leave the area. On my way back through the equipment room I hit the stop button on the operating unit converter in a futile attempt to cut off electricity in the operations center.

Someone, I don't know who, had already set off the fire alarm. I ran upstairs to the second floor and again

Illustration 28.
Damage inside the
Fresno State (now
University) computer
installation from fire
bomb thrown through
unprotected window,
May 19, 1970

Illustration 29.
Damage to interior of
computer building from
bomb set outside the
building by militant
students, University of
Kansas, Lawrence,
December 11, 1970

hollered to clear the building. I came back down and started herding people out of the building. I went outside as the fire trucks started arriving. Two firemen were running toward the windows where smoke was pouring out and flames were visible. The firemen had water type extinguishers, and I hollered at them that it was an electrical fire. I am not sure if they had already sprayed water into the flames or not. The firemen then applied a chemical extinguisher to the flames. A security officer arrived, and I entered the building with him.[10]

A photograph of some of the damage in the Fresno State computer center appears in Illustration 28.

Damage from wire cutters and acid

Various techniques have been used in militant attacks. Vandals damaged an IBM 360/40 computer at Boston University in March 1969 by using wire cutters (pliers) and acid. In this case militants cut connecting wires and threw acid into printed circuits of the computer.

Powerful explosives have been used in other attacks, as at the University of Kansas and at the Army Mathematics Research Center at the University of Wisconsin.

Holding the computer hostage

The technique used in some student confrontations has been to seize the installation, and to announce thereafter that the computer was being held "hostage" until seemingly nonnegotiable demands of the students were met. An IBM installation at Brandeis University was held in this manner until the administration agreed to demands. A somewhat similar "computer kidnapping" was used by militant activists at Northwestern University.

Other student groups have occupied university and college installations, some being expelled without serious incident. In at least two of these incidents, it was found after eviction that fire bombs had been strategically planted near the computer console, but that the bombs had not gone off.

[9] "Firebombs Damage a Computer Center," *The Office*, August 1970, p. 42.

1.

Does the public have knowledge of the location and functions of the computer installation?

2.

Are public tours allowed? How are they supervised?

3.

Does the computer belong to a firm or institution that is considered a part of "the establishment"?

4.

Are hiring practices such that militants would be screened out and eliminated from job consideration?

5.

Is awareness of responsibility on the part of employees a part of the overall plan for security?

6.

Is physical security sufficient to keep out militants, if employees discharge duties in a proper manner?

14 THE STORAGE AND USE OF MAGNETIC TAPES AND DISCS

Storage of data and programs on punched cards, magnetic tapes, discs, or drums is a major and vital function of any computer operation. In almost all computer installations one can find this kind of storage. The devices of concern in this chapter are those in common use—magnetic tapes and discs which can be removed from the computer upon completion of use.

Magnetic data media can represent concentrations of a large amount of data. For example, a 2400-foot reel of magnetic tape can contain over 40 million characters of data. Removable magnetic discs can contain from 3 to 40 million characters of data, depending on the design.

The ability to store such a great amount of data on a small physical device is both a liability and an asset. It is a liability in that destruction of such a storage device results in the loss of a great amount of data. Additionally, magnetic tapes and discs must be provided with a suitable environment if they are to perform properly. Otherwise, loss of stored data may occur.

Further, magnetic tapes and discs have a limited lifetime of use under normal operating conditions. Computer operations personnel must understand the environment and procedures needed in order to successfully utilize magnetic tapes and discs, or loss of data may result. The relation of magnetic tapes and discs to overall computer system security is direct. Loss of vital EDP data is just as real from mishandling as from outright theft.

Storage

Magnetic tapes and discs that are not in use are commonly stored in a tape library. Depending on the goals of the installation, the storage area or tape library should meet a number of different criteria.

The temperature and humidity of the storage location or tape library should be similar to the normal temperature and humidity in the computer room. The tape library should also be a clean environment, with no smoking or food consumption allowed in the area.

Requirements for fire protection vary from site to site, and the threat of fire has been covered in detail in Chapter 4. However, there are a number of important items that should be emphasized in conjunction with fire protection for the tape library. No combustible materials, such as data cards, forms, or trash should ever be stored or allowed to accumulate in the tape library. All storage shelves and furnishings should be made of metal or other noncombustible materials. Economics should dictate the extent of fire protection that is to be employed. If suitable fire protection is justified, design and construction measures should be taken to provide the tape library with fire-resistant walls, ceilings, and floors. Some data simply may not be of sufficient value to warrant extensive protection from fire, provided vital information is backed up.

The threat of data destruction by magnets was covered in detail in Chapter 12. However, it is well to point out again that no magnetic devices, such as magnetic door latches, magnetized flashlights, or magnetized memo holders, be allowed in the tape library. Additionally, if a bulk magnetic tape erasing device is used in the facility, it should not be located in the tape library. This is to prevent the convenient destruction of the tape library by a saboteur.

If the installation is located where electromagnetic radiation from radio frequency emitters, such as radars or communication transmitters, may damage magnetic data media, then shielding of the tape library should be considered.

Physically, the tape library area must offer controlled access. This area must be capable of being locked up to prevent unauthorized access to the stored data, and access to the tape library must be available only to authorized operations personnel. Commonly, the responsibility for operation of the tape library is handled by an employee who is designated as the "tape librarian." All movement of tapes and discs from and to the library are authorized and carried out by the librarian. It is imperative that access to the library be restricted only to authorized individuals. Failure to enforce access restrictions to the tape library virtually negates the protective value of the library.

Storage techniques

Magnetic tape should be stored in dust-proof plastic cannisters designed to support the reel by its hub. The hub is the strongest point of support for the reel and is, of course, the point of attachment to the tape drive itself. Even though the cannisters may be stacked, it is preferable to store them in racks designed specifically for tape cannister storage. Additionally, the loose end of the tape should be secured with either a vinyl strip or a hold-down sponge. All tapes in the library should be file protected; that is, stored without a "file protect" ring. Only scratch tapes should be stored with a file protect ring.

Time should be taken to store magnetic discs in the containers provided by the manufacturer. Here again, metal storage racks are available to hold magnetic discs in their containers. There should be a firm rule that magnetic discs are not removed from their protective containers except to be mounted for use upon the disc drive.

Tape library procedures

Several basic procedures should be followed in the operation of the tape library. Since the tape librarian is responsible for the issuance and receiving of magnetic tapes and discs, a procedure must be established that will properly account for their usage. When a user submits a job to be run, he will normally specify what tapes and discs will be needed. At the time of job submittal, the user and operator should sign a four-part form indicating who submitted the job, who accepted it, and what tapes and discs are required. The form must have been previously signed by the individual who authorized the job. The user then retains one copy of the form for his records. When the job is actually run, the operator uses the form to authorize the withdrawal of tapes and discs from the tape library. Here again, the tape librarian signs the form and retains a copy for his own records. When the job is completed and the tapes are returned, the librarian signs the operator's copy, indicating that he returned the tapes and discs. Thus, each individual concerned has records that account for his actions. The fourth copy of the form is retained in a master file as an accounting record of computer system usage.

The tape librarian should maintain an inventory of all volumes in the library. He should be responsible to an auditing to determine that all volumes are accounted for. A labelling system should be designed that includes a label for the physical device and a label written magnetically on the tape itself. In this way, loss of the label from the tape reel will not preclude identification of the data. The librarian should also maintain records about the age and usage of magnetic tapes and discs.

The maintenance of magnetic tapes should be the responsibility of the tape librarian. With use, magnetic tapes accumulate dirt and receive wear, both of which can lead to errors when the tape is used. These errors are normally realized in the inability to recover all of the data originally written on the tape. Often, repeated attempts to read the tape will be met with success and the data will be recovered. Most computer systems are designed automatically to attempt to reread a magnetic tape a fixed number of times when such an error occurs. However, computer time is lost when magnetic tape read errors occur and, worse, the data may be lost altogether. Repeated use of the tape also causes wear, particularly on the part of the tape used in loading the volume on the tape drive. As a result, a program of periodic tape cleaning and inspection should be instituted. Many machines for cleaning and testing magnetic tapes are available. Illustration 30 shows

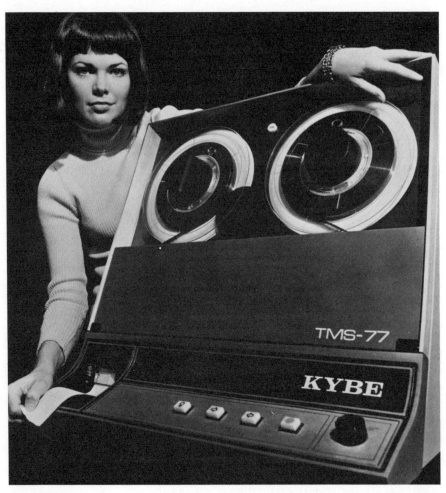

Illustration 30.
Photograph of a tape
cleaner/tester

182

such a machine. Such a device will clean the tape and then test it to determine where errors exist. After cleaning, tapes may be put back into service if they meet testing criteria. It may be possible to repair some tapes that fail to pass the testing phase, but if not, the tapes can be replaced. Such a testing program can be initiated when a tape has excessive read errors or when the tape has been used a set number of times. All data must be copied from a tape before cleaning and testing or it will be destroyed. A conscientious cleaning and testing program can give added data security to an installation. Loss of data from a saboteur's actions and from a defective magnetic tape are equally damaging. The tape librarian should be responsible for initiating the cleaning and testing of tapes. As with the bulk tape-erasing machine, the tape cleaner and tester should not be located in the tape library since it can be used to destroy data stored on magnetic tapes.

The computer room environment is critical to the life and well-being of magnetic tapes and discs. The computer room should be as clean as possible. No smoking, eating, or drinking should ever be tolerated in the machine room, as this can lead to contamination of equipment and magnetic data media with dirt and dirt-attracting residues. The computer room floor should be periodically cleaned with a no-residue cleaner. However, the floors should not be waxed. Operations personnel should be encouraged to wash their hands before entering the machine room after they have consumed food or drink. If possible, the computer room should be supplied with conditioned and filtered air at a slight positive pressure. Thus, air will always leave the room, preventing the entrance of dirt and dust.

Computer room procedures

Operations personnel should be trained in the correct manner of mounting magnetic tapes and discs. The exact procedure varies depending upon the manufacturer and design of the tape drive. However, a few basic rules are common to all. Tape reels should always be handled by the hub, never by the flanges. To mount the tape, pressure should be applied only to the hub. Care should be exercised in handling the leader of the tape. Operations personnel should be encouraged to strive for care in handling the tapes instead of speed. Likewise, when handling magnetic discs, the procedure recommended by the manufacturer should be employed. No attempt should ever be made to speed up the mounting or dismounting of disc packs from drives.

Magnetic tapes and discs should be transported from the tape library to the machine room on carts designed for that purpose. They should not be stacked carelessly or carried around under arm. Magnetic tapes and discs should never be stacked on equipment, as heat damage and a resultant loss of data may occur. A proper cart allows for the convenient transportation of tapes and discs to and from the library, as well as providing a work area from which to load the tape drives and store the empty cannisters.

The procedures used to mount and dismount magnetic tapes and discs should be periodically monitored. It is only too easy for personnel to become lax in this area.

Transportation of magnetic data media

Magnetic data media should be packaged in cannisters for tapes and the proper container for discs —the proper container being that supplied by the manufacturer. In order to protect the shipment from stray magnetism, a minimum of three inches of spacing between the data media and the outside of the shipping crate should be maintained. This spacing can be insured by packing material.

Cleaning of magnetic data media

Regular cleaning of magnetic tape and disc drives should be part of standard operational procedures. Magnetic tape drive heads and rollers should be cleaned to prevent the accumulation and spread of dirt and oil from and to tapes. Normally, operations personnel can perform this job without assistance from maintenance personnel. Cleaning of dust and dirt from surfaces of the tape drive unit should also be accomplished.

Normally, cleaning of disc drives is done less frequently than tape drives since the units are enclosed. Usually, the cleaning of disc drives must be accomplished by qualified maintenance personnel.

1.
Is the amount of data stored on magnetic tapes and discs known?

2.
Does the tape library meet the environmental, fire protection, and security design goals?

3.
Is the role of the tape librarian well defined? Does he have absolute authority over the operation of the tape library?

4.
Are magnetic tapes stored in cannisters which support the tape reel by its hub? Are magnetic disc packs stored in the manufacturer recommended containers?

5.
Do operational procedures exist to provide for the issuance and receiving of tapes and discs from the tape library?

6.
Does a program exist for the cleaning and testing of magnetic tapes?

7.
Is the computer room maintained as a clean environment?

8.
Are operations personnel properly trained in the correct procedures for mounting and dismounting magnetic tapes and discs?

15

EMERGENCY SHUTDOWN AND DISASTER PLANNING

Computer centers often follow routines from day to day, intent on processing and current schedules, ignoring the problems that could arise during an emergency. But it is unrealistic to assume that the routine may continue indefinitely. Management must expect to be forced sometimes to cope with the unexpected or the unknown. Practical planning, then, should take this into account.

In case of fire, the damage to the computer may be increased considerably if the computer cannot be de-energized. Then too, there is always a possibility that a live electrical line could result in the electrocution of someone fighting the fire. One of the problems in the much-publicized Pentagon fire of 1959 was the fact that fire broke out in locations that prevented employees from reaching the electrical power switch. Prior to that time the need for a second emergency shutdown button outside the operating room had not been foreseen. Today, this is one of the emergency planning precautions recommended by the National Fire Protection Association.

In this connection, it is frequently observed that the shutdown button in a computer room is located in such a position that employees may brush against it, or so that a cleaning employee could accidentally strike it with a mop handle or other object.

It is essential that this button be easily accessible to supervision. However, it should be protected against accidental shutdown of power. A protective shield that extends out from the wall will give protection to the button and will still allow easy access.

To illustrate what may happen unless the shutdown button is protected: In a recent case in Los Angeles a computer operator stumbled and fell against the button, bringing the computer to a halt and causing loss. Locating the shutdown button at a height of six feet six inches would have made it more inaccessible, but easy to reach.

In spite of the modern glass and poured concrete construction of today's business buildings, there is still a possibility of fire. Holes left in the walls for gas and electric lines may allow flames to spread from area to area. Air conditioning equipment and elevator shafts may add to the problem. Trash, paper stocks, furniture, carpeting, and drapes may provide fuel, as has been previously pointed out. Then too, high-voltage electrical lines, explosive gas fumes, volatile chemicals, and corrosive acids may be found in any industrial area or in some large buildings. Training drills may therefore be desirable for the business as a whole, coordinated with the individual needs of the data processing center.

To illustrate what may happen when there is no planning, consider the following description from an actual incident in a typical office building: Numerous employees, obviously frightened, left their assigned work areas and rushed to jam stairways and elevator lobbies. An elderly woman slipped and fell on the stairs, bowling ten other employees into a heap at a stair landing. Elevator doors would not open, and one employee screamed loudly as she beat both fists against the elevator doors. Arriving on the scene shortly after, firemen could find no one at the building entrance to direct them. Valuable time was lost before they could learn which floors of the building were involved.

To avoid this type of incident, specific procedures should be worked out for emergency situations. Management responsibility should be fixed, with a chain of command. This is because plans developed and adopted in advance will insure the continuance of purposeful direction and leadership. Planning will protect employees, will minimize damage to physical facilities and assets, and will enable a return to normal computer operations at the earliest possible moment.

It is desirable for a computer center of almost any size to have a management committee, capable of

Planning committee

taking over the programming and operations of the computer in case of a serious emergency.

But this takeover would assume that the computer installation was still physically intact, and was not threatened by fire, flood, riot, or other disaster. To cope with potential damage to the computer, it is recommended that a separate emergency planning committee be set up. The objective of this committee should be to provide overall planning, administration, and implementation as a basis for organized action in case of a disaster. In most firms or institutions it has been found that such a committee should delegate responsibility and authority to division or department heads. Besides adopting necessary polices and preparing written directives, this committee should make certain there is acceptance of responsibilities and implementation of necessary details.

Coordinator

A committee is useful for planning and organization, but is seldom well suited for any kind of emergency action. One single official, a security coordinator or emergency coordinator, should immediately take charge on the scene of any potential disaster. Designation of an alternate coordinator is also recommended. Until an emergency actually arises, the coordinator's duties should include an evaluation of readiness in individual departments or sections. He may also oversee department heads in training employees for individual assignments.

Security officer

If there is a uniformed guard or security force at the computer facility, the emergency coordinator should make full use of the training and authority of these security officers. Then too, the chief security officer should have close relations with local police and fire officials. During the planning stage, all possible courses of action to be taken by security officers or uniformed guards should be reduced to writing.

As a practical matter, it is often found that the chief security officer may be off duty at the time of an emergency. A chain of command should be followed in the security organization at all times, to avoid delay in notifying police and fire authorities, and in initiating first aid or rescue action.

Steps should also be taken in advance to provide emergency equipment for the security officer or building engineer. It is suggested that access be available to a fireman's ax, a large pry bar, a respirator, a self-contained breathing apparatus, portable lighting equipment, flashlights, a bomb blanket, an asbestos fire suit, and emergency firearms. The needs here would, of course, vary greatly, depending on the size of the building, the number of employees, and other factors. **Emergency equipment and medical aid**

If the facility is large enough to utilize the services of a trained nurse or medical station, this aspect should also be included in the emergency plans. In the absence of the nurse during night hours, it is suggested that the uniformed guard force or engineer have access to the medical office and supplies. If there are no employees with first-aid training during night hours, then consideration should be given to training shift supervisors, guards, or building engineers. Courses in first aid are regularly taught by the American Red Cross, and these classes include instruction on basic first aid in case of burns or electrocution.

If there are a number of employees in the engineering and maintenance departments, it is suggested that some or all of these employees be organized as a fire brigade. Training in this regard can almost always be furnished by a city or county fire department.

Among specific duties to be assigned during an emergency, it is important that a building employee be stationed on the street, to direct fire and police patrols to the specific location of the emergency problem. This is essential if the structure has a number of floors, or the building is unusually large.

Many modern buildings are completely dark in the event of a power failure, and can be quite hazardous. It is therefore desirable that there be automatic emergency lighting systems (units) in appro- **Emergency lighting** priate locations in the computer installation. It is also worth noting that employees sometimes "borrow" flashlights or misplace equipment. Since emergency lighting systems usually require some periodic maintenance, it is desirable to test emergency lighting systems regularly.

Check lists and dry runs

Emergency check lists should be prepared in advance, and maintained in a location where they are certain to be handy in time of need, available to the coordinator and department heads.

It is recommended that the coordinator supervise regular test runs of emergency plans, with employees acting out their specific assignments. Simulated drills will result in critical evaluation and improved planning and execution. This testing will increase employee familiarity with problems, will prevent panic in an actual emergency, and will reveal undisclosed problems that may not have been considered during the planning stage.

Removal of software

While the computer proper (the processor) is of great value, it may be easier to replace than computer software. In most instances the computer manufacturers would be able to rush replacement hardware to the scene of a disaster. But some tapes or discs may well be virtually irreplaceable.

Some computer centers have successfully removed vital tapes, discs, or records from the premises in time of emergency by use of a wheeled records cart. Small enough to be easily pushed by a female employee, but large enough to hold a number of essential tapes or discs, these carts may be stored in the business vault in riot-prone locations.

The technique here is to have employees quickly place the vital tapes or discs into the cart, locking the doors if the cart is lockable. The cart can then be pushed to the nearest freight or receiving dock and rolled onto the bed of any available company truck. The truck can then be driven completely out of the neighborhood, to a place of safety.

This procedure can be used if floodwaters are approaching, if fire breaks out at a nearby location, or if a riot seems likely.

Of course, if the computer center has a vault with an adequate fire rating, it will often be satisfactory to rely on the protection afforded by the vault. In the event of a riot, however, experience shows that members of a mob may not concentrate all their efforts toward looting or carrying away appliances, furniture, liquor, or merchandise. Past experience indicates rioters may also attempt to break into vaults or safes, intending to destroy records of accounts receivable. Rioters may then be able to avoid payment for purchases made on the installment plan.

In most instances it is of considerable importance to return the computer center to normal as soon as possible following an emergency. All priorities may be directed toward this objective. The availability of computer and building engineers, as well as maintenance employees, is considered essential in the period immediately following the emergency. Stopgap repairs and permanent restoration may both be requirements of the program. Planning should take into account those activities necessary to assess and repair damage, and to restore communications, utilities, and transportation services quickly. It is suggested that up-to-date telephone numbers and home addresses of all computer employees be maintained in a secure place, so that contacts can be made when the emergency comes to an end. If the computer operation is a large one, it may be necessary to instruct rank-and-file workers to return to duty, and to seek replacements for those who decline to return.

Returning to normal

If the emergency should occur a short time before payday, employees may sometimes be in financial difficulty. If the shutdown has extended for a considerable period of time, it may be found that some employees have accepted other employment. Others may not have the funds to return to work until finances are straightened out. Accordingly, it may be advisable to obtain funds for emergency loans to employees. Most employees can manage their financial affairs when paid on a regular basis, but are unable to do so in the event of usual developments.

Planning for bomb threats

In recent years some computer installations have been the object of bomb threats on more than one occasion. A large number of these attacks have been directed against university and banking computer centers, but others have involved business establishments. Figures indicate that in recent years nine out of ten major U.S. firms have been threatened with bombings.

While there are exceptions, in most cases the explosive charge has not been set to go off without advance warning. Most of these warnings have been given by anonymous telephone calls. If telephone operators are given some advance training, they may be able to extract some information from the caller as to the specific area where the device has been planted.

For instance, the operator may say something like the following: "Wait a minute! There are children going on a tour through our building this afternoon. You wouldn't want them to get hurt, would you? Can you tell me what part of the building to keep them out of?"

Or the operator may be able to ask another type of question, such as, "Do you mean the device is planted in our main building on Center Street? Or is it in the new computer location on Broadway?"

This last question may be a ruse to determine whether the call is a false alarm, since there is no company building on Broadway street. With a definite indication as to the location or as to whether the call is a false alarm, management may be able to determine whether evacuation should be undertaken and where a search should be made.

Keeping the bomb outside

It is difficult to plant a bomb inside a computer location if good physical controls are enforced. That is an additional reason why access should be so carefully limited.

192

If the computer center is closed and adequately locked at night, it may not be easy for an intruder to gain access. Night hours are frequently selected by bomb attackers, however, as the militants want to cause destruction when there is little possibility that employees may be working. If employees are on duty, there is a greater chance of immediate detection.

It is usually easier to gain entry into a business building during working hours. That is why receptionists and maintenance employees should be alert to control and regulate the activities of outsiders, especially those carrying wrapped packages or bundles.

After a bomb threat call has been received, the emergency coordinator for the computer center must make a difficult decision. A policy that calls for the automatic evacuation of all employees from the building can be so expensive that it is almost prohibitive. On the other hand, the threat against the lives of programmers, operators, and other employees may be very real. If the telephone operator or other employee receiving the warning call is fortunate enough to develop information that will localize the danger area, then the amount of computer downtime may be considerably reduced. But EDP management cannot simply ignore an announced intention to blow up the building, the computer, or the employees, even though the great majority of all such calls will prove to be false.

The decision to evacuate

Evacuation is not only expensive, but may be a complicated procedure if the complex is part of a large building or business complex. In a crowded metropolitan area, as much as 30 minutes may be needed to notify occupants and completely evacuate employees.

The decison to evacuate or to continue computer operations may seldom be taken lightly, and may vary from case to case in the same building. In the final analysis, however, it must be a combination of moral judgment, good common sense, and practical business. One aspect to be kept in mind by management is that if a false call results in prolonged business interruption, then there is an increased possibility that other threatening calls can be anticipated in the future.

Searching for the bomb

If there actually is a bomb in the computer center, it is essential that employees be gotten out of the building as soon as possible. In searching for a bomb, however, there are no other individuals who have such intimate knowledge of the building as employees. They can usually tell at a glance whether something in their work area has been disturbed or whether a strange object has been left there. For all their intimate knowledge of their work areas, however, employees should never be forced to conduct such a search. Participation should be completely voluntary.

It is in the search operation that advance preparations by the emergency planning committee will show to advantage. Plans for individual floors and for each room of the building should be obtained in advance, with likely areas of concealment predetermined. Search responsibility should be fixed in detail, but with employees participating on a voluntary basis. Here again, a drill prior to the emergency may prove of value.

In conducting the search, a portable, hand-held metal detector may be helpful in locating bombs with containers made of metal pipe or those containing large metal parts. These detecting devices are limited in range, however, and the practicality of these detectors is doubtful in many searches. Also, there is no certainty that the bomb will be encased in metal.

Other search equipment may be needed, including flashlights and short ladders. From the experience of past cases, the most likely places for bomb concealment include public restrooms, janitorial and service closets, air conditioning ducts, and elevator shafts.

If a bomb is found

No time should be lost in evacuating the immediate area around an object that appears to be a bomb. The explosive device, or suspected object, should never be moved or touched by computer center personnel. This is best left for the police or fire department bomb squad.

Bombs of any kind are extremely unpredictable, especially homemade devices. Extreme caution should be exercised, even though the bomb threat call may have specified a definite time for detonation. The device could be triggered by tugging on anything protruding from the package. Also, computer personnel should be warned against attempts to deactivate a dangerous device by lowering it into a bucket of water. This may have the opposite effect, as the water may act as a carrier of electricity to complete the circuit that sets off the explosive charge.

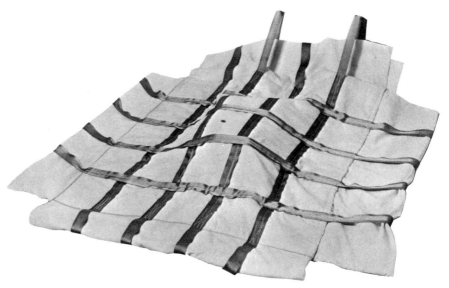

Illustration 31.
A commercial bomb blanket

Illustration 31 shows a bomb blanket that is sold commercially. It is sometimes utilized to cover a bomb or suspected object. Made of several layers of special, nylon ballistic material used for body armor and military applications, these blankets have proved quite effective in reducing damage caused by bomb fragmentation. Made to be easily carried by one individual, these bomb blankets are helpful but should be used only with appropriate caution.

The emergency bomb plan of some large computer installations includes a procedure in which trained security guards place sandbags around the suspected device in order to reduce damage. Where this procedure is followed, filled sandbags may be stockpiled near an outside guard post or near the maintenance engineer's office.

It is usually recommended by bomb experts that building doors and windows in the vicinity of the suspected bomb be left open. In many explosions, physical damage has been less in those locations where this procedure has been followed.

Consideration should be given to a requirement in the disaster plan that someone be designated to cut off electrical power and the natural gas supply. This should not be done, of course, if it will expose an employee to danger. If this action can be taken before a bomb is detonated, it will usually help to prevent the spread of fire. As a word of caution, it may not be advisable to cut off power to building elevators until it is certain that evacuation is complete. Meanwhile, employees experienced in handling extinguishers or fire fighting equipment should maintain safe positions near the available equipment. If there is any question, they should remain well out of reach of the explosive device.

Check off list

1.
Are there written plans for emergency shutdown?

2.
Have the plans been tested for workability under simulated conditions?

3.
Is the plan directed by an emergency coordinator?

4.
Are there written instructions and assignments for

(a) telephone operators, (b) security personnel and/or uniformed guards, (c) engineering and maintenance personnel, and (d) nursing and medical personnel?

5.
Is a records handcart always available for emergency removal of records, tapes, and discs?

6.
Are there written procedures for getting the facility back into operation as soon as possible?

7.
Have plans been made for employee evacuation if a bomb is discovered?

8.
If a bomb should be found, do employees understand how to protect personnel and property?

16

LEGAL PROTECTION FOR THE COMPUTER

A great number of computer services and types of equipment are now available to the potential user. While most manufacturers and suppliers are completely legitimate, there are some who utilize standard form contracts that drastically limit responsibility by the supplier. Some go so far as to excuse the manufacturer or supplier for negligence. Phillip J. Scaletta, Jr., of the faculty of Purdue University warns that:

> Too often these lease contracts are patterned after standard machinery lease contracts using the standard boiler plate clauses covering terms of payment, warranty, patents, title, installation charges, accessory charges, engineering charges. They do not take into consideration the problems inherent in the computer operation which are not present in the ordinary lease of machinery for manufacturing uses.[1]

In leasing or buying a computer it may be well to obtain competent legal advice during the selection and evaluation process. Any contract that is negotiated should be fair to both parties. At the outset, it is suggested that a contract file be set up, with complete documentation retained to support all developments.

It is not uncommon to find that a company spends a considerable amount of time preparing suitable contracts on company automobiles, equipment, and office forms. On the other hand, the same firm will often sign a contract for computer equipment involving large sums of money, even though this standard contract furnished by the supplier fails to specify a level of performance the user may rely on.

---

[1] Phillip J. Scaletta, Jr., "Legal Ramifications of the Computer," reprinted by Charles F., Jr., and John M. Hemphill, with permission from the November 1970, issue of *Data Management*, published by the Data Management Assn., 505 Busse Highway, Park Ridge, Ill. 60068.

William D. Lang, Jr. has suggested that the following rules be incorporated into a data processing
contract:

**Contracts for
equipment**

State what standards of performance are expected
and which constitute satisfactory performance for hardware, programs, or services. Also, what criteria will be
used to determine if compliance with the standards has
been adhered to before certifying to satisfactory performance on the part of the supplier.

Establish milestones to measure performance and adherence to standards. The milestone should be established so as to allow sufficient time for obtaining
alternative services if cancellation of the contract is
deemed necessary.

Specify what remedies the user may obtain for
"breach of contract," loss of use of the equipment, negligence on the part of the supplier, and an opportunity
for remedy should the agreement be terminated by
either party.[2]

Firms and institutions frequently incur legal responsibilities by leasing or purchasing some of the
so-called "commercial canned software packages"
that are used to operate the computer. Commonly,
the buyer or leasor of these packages is under a legal
obligation not to reproduce the package or to let
other parties have the use of it. As a part of the sales
or leasing agreement, there may be contractual
penalties attached that should be pointed out to
employees. If this is done, employees will almost
always be inclined to handle the package in a secure
manner.

Contract restrictions

Some products and services of modern-day business and industry tend to become more specialized
from year to year. Much of the true worth of these
products and services is reflected in their unique
features, achieved through the expenditure of considerable time and money in research and development projects. The desire to protect the intangible
assets represented by these new products and ser-

Program protection

[2] William D. Lang, Jr., "Get It In Writing," reprinted
from *Administrative Management*, © Geyer-McAllister
Publications, Inc., August 1971, p. 12.

vices is the continuing responsibility of management.

It is here that competent legal advice should be sought out. A lawyer is often called upon to furnish advice to his client, based on his ability to locate and interpret prior cases that have been appealed through the courts. Businessmen need to know that they can plan their affairs, secure in the knowledge that decided cases will represent protective law for the future.

When a whole new area of technology is developed, as in the computer field, untested areas of law may be opened up. Decided cases are not available to serve as a basis for the lawyer's opinion. Gradually, however, some of the old legal principles are applied to the new problems. As time goes by, basic rights are clarified and respected by the courts. There is still much to be settled in the field of computer law, but guideposts have evolved to assist the legal profession in furnishing predictable protection.

It should be clearly understood that the material which follows is not directed toward enabling the computer user to dispense with competent legal advice. This would prove a questionable economy in many instances.

There are three broad areas in which legal assistance can be valuable in protecting company or institutional assets. An additional area, that of patentability of computer programs, has been struck down by the U.S. Supreme Court. Patent protection for computer programs will therefore be dependent upon the enactment of new laws by Congress. Areas that are now available include:

1. Legal protection for computer data on the basis that it merits trade secret protection,
2. Legal protection afforded by federal copyright laws, and
3. Protection by setting up adjudication procedures for settling disputes; by developing industry-wide ethics; and by additional legislation.

Treating computer files and programs as trade
secrets appears to provide the best possibility for
legal protection, in most instances.

A trade secret has been legally defined as a "confidential formula, pattern, device, or compilation of
information which is used in one's business, and
which gives the owner an opportunity to obtain an
advantage over competitors who do not have it."[3]

Simply put, a trade secret is proprietary information that gives business a "head start" over
competitors.

The courts have always held that new industrial
and technical developments belong to society as a
whole. To hold otherwise would be to obstruct the
well-being of the general public. On the other hand,
if a private company cannot reap individual rewards
from the results of scientific and engineering experiments, then there is slight incentive to develop and
utilize new ideas or processes.

The problem here is that the law does not afford
the same protection to trade secrets that is given to
prevent theft of company merchandise in the ware-
house. As distinguished from other kinds of company valuables, the holder of a trade secret does not
actually own a property right in it at all. Rather, he
has only the right to keep others from taking the
trade secret from him in an unfair and improper
way. Under the usually accepted ideas of larceny, it
is necessary for the owner or his agent to be deprived of possession as well as of use of the article
in question. If a thief duplicates and sells a secret
chemical formula, for instance, he has deprived the
owner of neither possession nor use of the formula.
The harm sustained, however, may be just as great
as if the owner had completely lost the secret.

A competitor, working independently, may man-

[3] Restatement of Torts, 757 Comment (b) (1939). A trade
secret was defined by the court in *Victor Chemical Works* v.
Iliff, 299 Ill. 532; 132 N. E. 806, as "A plan or process, tool
mechanism, or compound known only to its owner and those
of his employees to whom it is necessary to confide it."

age to duplicate a secret formula or process. In doing so, the competitor acquires the same right as the original holder. So long as the discoverer maintains his confidential process or information as a secret, then he is entitled to the protection of the laws relating to unfair competition.

The courts, however, are reluctant to limit the rights of employees to make a living. Basic standards of freedom of employment allow a worker to transfer the skills of his profession whenever he accepts employment with a competitor's company. Nevertheless, trade secrets, if kept secret by the company from its competition, may be claimed as corporate property. Data banks, for example, that were compiled by a computer company at great expense, are entitled to protection. Another firm working from basic sources, may compile exactly the same information. If the data is copied and sold by an unethical employee, however, money damages may be awarded against the wrongful purchaser. In addition, in some instances a court may issue an injunction prohibiting the wrongful purchaser from using the information that had been protected as a trade secret. A court-enforced accounting of profits may also be obtained.

Milton R. Wessel has pointed out in *Harvard Business Review* that six tests are usually applied by the courts before they will protect computer programs and data as trade secrets. As noted, in part, by Mr. Wessel, these tests are:

1. Is the program really secret?

It might seem redundant to say that a trade secret must be secret; . . . The ease with which the data can be obtained from their holder may furnish a valid defense. . . .

Be sure that programs are kept under lock and key with access limited to those who must see or use them. . . .

Boldly stamp all programs and documents. . . .

If programs must be loaned as part of the business . . . keep a record of such disclosures, and have the outsider execute a written commitment not to reveal the information to anyone else. . . .

2. Is the program really valuable?

. . . The best tangible evidence of value is proof of the use of the program. . . .

Make an entry showing each time the program is run and the name of the customer. . . .

3. Was the program developed and owned by the company? . . .

The job description of any employee who helps to develop a program should include some phase of program design as part of his work. . . .

Second, if the program is produced by a team effort, that fact should be made clear. . . .

4. Was it difficult to develop the program?

. . . The log should therefore contain as much detail as possible to record the blood, sweat, and tears devoted to the effort. . . .

5. Has the program been copied? . . .

Proof of similarity is obviously an important link in the chain of evidence establishing trade secret infringement. . . .

One method might be to give related programs a proprietary name. If the name chosen is, say, Procam 1, Procam 2, Procam 3, and so on, minor adjustments from customer to customer can be identified by letters such as Procam 3a, Procam 3b, and Procam 3c.

With records of this kind, a company will have a much easier time convincing a court that Procam 5 was a direct descendant of Procam 2, . . .

6. Is it fair to protect the program? . . .

Every effort should be made to limit the impact of any restrictions on employees in order to avoid unnecessary interference with their opportunities for employment elsewhere in the industry. . . .[4]

In order to put employees on notice, it is generally advisable to request them to sign restrictive agreements not to reveal trade secrets. The type of agreement needed will vary from computer center to computer center, and it is beyond the scope of this work to become involved in legal details.

[4] Milton R. Wessel, "Legal Protection of Computer Programs," *Harvard Business Review*, March–April 1965, pp. 97–105.

Copyright registration

Article 1, Section 8, of the United States Constitution gives Congress the right: "To promote the Progress of Science and useful Arts, by securing for limited Times to Authors and Inventors the exclusive Right to their respective Writings and Discoveries;"

For several years, however, the United States Copyright Office declined to process computer programs for copyright registration. In May 1964 this policy was reversed, and computer programs were declared capable of registration.

Two basic problems have long bothered copyright officials as to whether a computer program satisfied the requirements of the federal law. These questions are:

1. To satisfy the law a computer program as such must be the "writing of an author," and
2. To comply with statutory requirements, a reproduction of the program in a form actually used to operate or be "read" by the computer is a "copy" that is acceptable for registration.

Based on prior court decisions, the copyright office has pointed out that: "Both of these are doubtful questions. However, in accordince with its policy of resolving doubtful issues in favor of registration whenever possible, the copyright office will consider registration for a computer program if certain requirements have been met."[5]

Problems arise here as to whether the program is still the readable work of an author, once it has been reduced to punch card form, when it has been translated into machine language, and when it is neither readable nor visible to the eye when transferred to discs or magnetic tape.

An old case that was decided in 1908 (*White–Smith Music Publishing Company* v. *Appollo Company*, 209 U.S. 1) seems to hold against the registration of computer programs. This case, how-

[5] Copyright office circular #31D, April 1967.

ever, involved copyright registration for the paper roll of an old-style player piano, and there seem to be considerable differences in the facts. Attorney Henry W. Hope, an authority on copyright and patent law, writing in the *Texas Bar Journal*, ventured the opinion that the courts will eventually uphold copyright protection for computer programs. Hope added that a number of legal problems related to this conclusion are still in doubt.[6]

In effect, it appears that the decision of the copyright office to accept programs for registration was to leave the way open for future judicial determinations as to the applicability of this type of legal protection.

While copyright registration could furnish legal protection to a number of firms, it would be of doubtful value to others. This is because the copyright law requires public disclosure of the program at the time of registration. In many instances this disclosure may be harmful.

Patentability

For a number of years there was doubt as to whether a computer program was patentable under Title 35 of the United States Code, Sections 101–3.

Early court decisions cast doubt as to the patentability. In a relatively recent line of cases, beginning with *In re Prater & Wei*, 415 Federal Second 1393 (decided in 1969) the U.S. Court of Customs and Patent Appeals indicated that a process is patentable if the applicant does not assert a claim to the same process if actually performed mentally.

In late 1972 the Supreme Court of the United States ruled, however, that program systems known as "software" are not patentable under present law. The Supreme Court took the approach that a program was essentially a series of mathematical calculations or mental steps, and that the two employees of Bell Telephone Laboratories who were seeking

---

[6] A detailed analysis of these legal problems is set out in an article by Henry W. Hope, "Computer Program Protection," *Texas Bar Journal*, January 1971, pp. 35–40, 53.

the patent had no right to "preempt the mathematical formula."[7]

This court decision, however, still leaves the possibility that Congress could pass legislation setting up requirements for patentability of computer programs.

New legislation

Organization throughout the computer industry could lead to new legislation that could provide better security to computer programs. Small firms, of course, cannot afford to sponsor such legislation on their own initiative. It would appear to be a field for organized action.

Code of ethics

It could also prove beneficial if an industry-wide code of ethics were written for the protection of computer programs and other sensitive data. Wide acceptance of such a code could reduce the number of disputes between companies and employees who have accepted positions with competing firms. This could furnish guidelines for hiring practices, and would serve to guide the courts as to what is acceptable in the industry. A code of ethics would also guide employees as to the type of conduct that is unacceptable from a professional standpoint.

Check off list

1.
Do contracts with computer manufacturers and suppliers specify standards of performance that must be met?

2.
Does the computer center treat confidential information in such a way that it will be given the legal protection that may be extended to "trade secrets"?

3.
Do employees understand that they may subject their employer to lawsuits if they allow unauthorized persons to copy or use restricted "commercial canned software packages"?

4.
Should copyright protection be considered for sensitive computer programs?

[7] See Thomas L. Chrisman, "Patentability of Computer Programs," *Texas Bar Journal*, January 1971, p. 33.

INSURANCE TO PROTECT THE COMPUTER

17

The fragile nature of all computer media is, of course, well recognized. This lack of physical durability may contribute to the ease with which an unprotected installation may be destroyed, and to the very large costs that may be expended in the recovery process. Complete loss of an uninsured computer center may stagger even a strongly financed business concern.

It has been previously stressed that a well-run prevention program avoids computer hazards whenever possible. Duplicate backup tapes and emergency standby equipment can be considered in much the same way as insurance, except that the approach used is to prevent loss, rather than to compensate after damage has occurred. This does not mean that insurance should ever be regarded as a substitute for good internal controls. Nevertheless, it is frequently observed in computer centers that insurance is viewed as a license to practice neglect, rather than as a means to hedge against catastrophe.

Special computer insurance was first offered by the Saint Paul Fire and Marine Insurance Company in 1961, as an aftermath of the Pentagon computer fire. Since that time, news publicity has been given to a number of instances of computer damage in which insurance was lacking. Some of these have involved very large sums of money.

A typical loss, but not necessarily the most expensive, involved the damage caused by the accidental breaking of an overhead fire sprinkler valve that dumped large quantities of water into several analog computers. The damage here was estimated at $127,000. In another instance a manufacturer lost $393,000 when a computer was struck by lightning and fire resulted. Another company was forced to spend $76,000 to reconstruct data that was destroyed when acid fumes from a nearby commercial installation filtered into the firm's tape library.

Some unusual losses

Insurance coverage
After several computer installations were damaged or destroyed by disasters, it became obvious to businessmen that available types of insurance were not adequate to the user's needs. This was especially so, since EDP media and equipment were generally excluded from coverage in some fire insurance policies. Gradually, new types of coverage were worked out to include specific risks to hardware, software, and other items. At first, there was a language barrier between insurance experts and data processing personnel, and computer insurance is still something of a specialized field.

Two approaches are taken by firms that offer insurance coverage for Electronic Data Processing. Some companies write specific policies for this kind of coverage, while others add new types of coverage to existing policy forms. In general, these policies are very complex from a layman's viewpoint, and require detailed study. Certain features of these policies should be known to members of management and officials who are responsible for the computer operation.

Equipment insurance
Data processing equipment insurance generally covers loss or damage to machines, wired panels, auxiliary equipment, special purpose equipment, air conditioning systems, and sometimes furniture. The hazards that may be covered include fire, explosion, building collapse, water damage, smoke, and accidental harm. Coverage may be given to specific pieces of equipment, and there are usually deductible provisions. Premiums for this kind of coverage vary considerably, depending upon building construction, exposure factors, and the value of the equipment.

While this is perhaps the most frequent kind of coverage, it may not be needed in some instances. One of the major U.S. computer manufacturers does not hold the user (lessee) responsible for loss or damage to leased hardware. Some other lease contracts that are in common use do not hold the user responsible for unintended damage, so long as the computer was housed in a building that conformed to the fire protection standards of the National Fire Protection Association. Still other lease contracts may exclude certain perils such as fire, while some contracts hold the user responsible only if damage was owing to the negligence of the user or his employees. This, of course, may be just the type of activity that the user wants protection against.

Some of the most costly losses that can be sustained at a computer installation may involve the destruction of data processing media. The coverage generally furnished here is for the cost of rebuilding data records damaged or ruined by fire, smoke, water, heat, building collapse, and other hazards. Most policies, however, do not include coverage here for accidental loss covered by operator errors, erasures, or "double punching."

Media insurance

In general, if no costs are agreed upon in advance, the insurance company will pay the actual cost of reconstructing data. Coverage will usually extend to any form of media—cards, tapes, disc packs, or memory rods.

Some policies utilize a valuable papers and records form. In order to assist in the reconstruction of damaged or destroyed media, this part of the policy may require that a duplicate copy of each master program or instruction tape be maintained in a vault or fireproof safe in a separate, outside location. This requirement, of course, makes it very important for management to be certain that the required backup data is kept in the off-site location at all times. If this is not done, then the entire policy, or specific clauses of the policy, may be void.

This kind of insurance is designed for those who process the data of others. Certified Public Accountants, computer service centers, banks that process data for other financial institutions, as well as some businesses, may find it prudent to carry some form of errors and omissions insurance. This type of coverage will repay the policyholder for honest mistakes made during work performed for

Errors and omissions insurance

outside clients. Some insurance firms will not accept coverage on consultants performing scientific, engineering, or mathematical calculations. There is considerable risk in covering such consultants, both from the possibility of an error or omission in their calculations, as well as from the professional advice they provide as consultants.

The insuring agreements and other policy provisions from a typical electronic data processor's errors and omissions policy are set out in the Appendix.

Business interruption insurance

This type of coverage applies to a loss in earnings that may result from specific perils, such as fire, flood, or building collapse. In order to collect on this portion of a policy, it is necessary to prove that a reduction in earnings has taken place. This does not cover the extra expense needed to get the system in operation after a disaster. This type of coverage does, however, protect against the loss of profits that resulted from shutdown.

Business interruption insurance may have considerable value in some instances. However, the real cost of a computer disaster to the business may sometimes be considerably more than that covered by loss-of-earnings coverage (business interruption insurance). No firm is insured against the loss of business momentum. When a company is closed down, even for a comparatively short time, customers frequently look to competitors for merchandise or service. The result may be damage to the competitive position, from which the business posture never completely recovers.

Extra-expense insurance

This class of coverage repays the extra expenses that may be needed to keep computer operations current following a breakdown. Normally, however, the direct costs of reconstruction of destroyed records is excluded.

The kind of expenses that are covered here include lease or rent from a temporary location, computer hardware and equipment rental, the salaries of additional employees, overtime pay expenses, extra costs for heat, light, and other utilities, and necessary travel expenses.

Insurance to repay any loss of accounts receivable may also be of value to some computer installations. Even if accounts receivable funds may be eventually paid, the temporary loss may necessitate borrowing capital to continue in business.

Loss of accounts receivable

Special indemnity bonds may be desirable in providing protection in some firms. A company comptroller, who has access to the computer, may be able to set up fictitious accounts. While there is no specific reason to mistrust a high official of this kind, a special indemnity bond may provide for the possibility of loss by embezzlement. This bond would provide coverage considerably in excess of company-wide coverages.

Special indemnity bonds

As an additional suggestion in connection with insurance, it is recommended that management consider directors' and officers' liability insurance. This would insure against personal responsibility in the event stockholders brought suit, claiming corporate losses because the directors or officers did not use proper security measures in operating and maintaining the company computer.

Directors and officers liability insurance

The cost of computer insurance comes about because of the concentration of valuable data and hardware in a comparatively small area. Insurance company executives frankly state that good security precautions at the computer center are among the factors that they consider in calculating premium costs.

Reducing insurance premiums

Among the specific items considered in figuring the insurance costs are:

1. The neighborhood environment in which the computer center is located;
2. The type of construction used in the building;
3. The likelihood of water damage;
4. Whether windows are located in outside walls;

5. What fire protection equipment is available, and whether carbon dioxide or Halon 1301 extinguishing systems are available;
6. Whether backup systems can take over in the event of failure of electricity, air-conditioning, or water supply;
7. The use and effectiveness of systems for regulating entry into the computer room, as well as the tape library;
8. Whether there is a workable disaster plan;
9. Whether there is adequate protection for backup tapes and discs; and
10. Whether repairs, such as welding, soldering, and painting are performed away from the computer center.

Insurance claims

Insurance authorities are in general agreement that more insurance claims by data processing installations result from water damage than from any other source. Frequently, these losses are due to flooding from rising streams, ruptured storm sewer lines, and broken water mains.

These claims seem to emphasize again the importance of choosing a location that is not susceptible to flooding.

PERSONAL PRIVACY AND
THE COMPUTER

The basic thrust of this book has been toward establishing protective systems for computers owned or operated to handle private business or institutional data. In recent years, the invasion of personal privacy by computers utilizing personal records in data banks has been an additional area of security concern.

Man has long been a hoarder of information. Since trade and commerce began, he has collected and analyzed essential knowledge. Today, as we know, business would be crippled without vast stores of data. Neither could the programs of society function without basic information regarding the needs of the individual man. No government can provide adequate services to the taxpayers without considerable personal background, especially since the citizens to today's world demand so much from their government.

So the collection of data and the maintenance of dossiers on private individuals or groups has not been something that began in recent times. But until a short time ago, it had never disturbed a significant number of people. Increased use of the computer, however, has brought new questions.

In itself, the computer is simply a new and more powerful tool. It has not actually caused any new invasion of privacy. Since information-gathering and record-keeping techniques have always been utilized, the computer's role in this regard is no different than a card index and steel filing cabinet system.

What is different is the computer's power to handle and interrelate large amounts of raw data. The efficiency and great speed of Electronic Data Processing has increased the ability to store, retrieve, and disseminate information to the level where the privacy of citizens may be invaded with relative ease. Before the computer was used, information had to be simplified and reduced to make it manageable in solving problems. Today, it is possible to use the same basic data many times over in the analysis of differing needs.

Privacy, in the sense that it is used here, could be defined as the legal or inherent right of persons or groups of persons to determine for themselves under what circumstances information about them will be communicated to others. The individual's desire for privacy, of course, is seldom absolute, as practically all men desire to participate in the activities of society to some extent.

The collection of information concerning private individuals has been made easier by the proliferation of record keeping in an increasingly bureaucratic society. Much of the information now in the possession of individual governmental agencies may be pooled into one central reservoir, a national data bank. A central file of this kind can absorb large batches of information about individuals, but it may be inadequately prepared to handle correction of input errors, or to keep information changes current. And unless errors are corrected, inaccurate data could harm any individual involved.

It is this background that has caused a number of individuals to question whether there are forces in the modern world that pose a threat to the privacy of information. Further, these writers reason that if such forces are uncontrolled, they will lead to totalitarianism that could threaten the freedom of all men.

There is valid reason to feel that if personal information falls into the wrong hands it could damage the lives of citizens and their families. For example, the file on an individual could contain wage and salary information, along with detailed personal history. It could include psychological and medical records as well, along with subjective evaluations of job performance. All of this could have a definite effect on the individual's ability to obtain better employment, to borrow money for a home mortgage, or to obtain personal credit.

A number of writers on this problem take the attitude that neither the government, a credit agency, nor anyone else should be allowed to collect or disseminate personal information without the permission of the individual involved. Commenting on this point of view and the movement associated with it, one magazine noted that this movement "is also rapidly becoming the biggest bandwagon of the decade, and there seems to be no end to the number of people prepared to jump onto it. . . . In America, and Europe too, there is indeed a witch-hunt. . . ."[1]

Of course, both sides to this argument agree that the computer community has a definite responsibility to the public to insure that unauthorized agencies or persons do not have access to personal information in the data bank. It is in deciding who has authority to use the data bank that there is considerable room for dispute. Safeguards should be built into the system, however, and data verification made against source documents.

On the other side of the picture, persons who buy on credit must expect that inquiry will be made into their past activities and habits. It can be argued that such persons have waived some of their right to privacy by applying for credit. A merchant or lending institution cannot be expected to risk capital unless there is sufficient information available to him to allow an intelligent appraisal of the credit risks. Likewise, a company that spends large amounts of money in employee training should not be forced blindly to hire individuals about whom nothing is known. In other cases, where an individual has been convicted repeatedly for serious crimes, it would work a hardship on society to refuse to furnish such information to the judge pass-

[1] "Computer File Privacy in Great Britain," *The Office*, September 1971, p. 41.

ing sentence, who might otherwise be persuaded to release the offender on probation.

But there is little dispute as to an individual's right to insist on adequate controls for the data bank. Whether there is an absolute right to privacy of all information may be subject to debate for some time to come.

CONCLUSION

There is no method available for measuring the quantity or quality of security that may be adequate for a computer. Perhaps there is no system that will always insure complete coverage. At best, security may be inconvenient and frequently time consuming. It requires the combined efforts of several levels of employees, some of whom may not even be acquainted with each other. And it is obvious that security cannot be measured like fuel for a gasoline tank, and pumped into a gasoline tank to keep the engine in operation. Even when all of the diverse elements work together in unity, there is no absolute assurance that all mishaps or accidents can be avoided. But most of the possibilities for loss can be eliminated, while damage from others may be minimized.

Whether we like it or not, security will remain an important business consideration. In many cases too little attention and too little money is allotted for computer security. On the other hand, there is always a possibility of being frightened into signing a contract for untested or impractical ideas or equipment, of little more value than a so-called "luck charm." Prior to making an investment of an unusual nature, it is recommended that management first avail itself of those basic deterrents and procedures that have proved effective in actual practice.

In the final analysis, management has little choice but to utilize whatever security seems reasonable, limited only by practical application and cost. To do otherwise is to jeopardize the very existence of the business or institution that relies on the computer.

BIBLIOGRAPHY

Periodicals

Adelson, Alan. "Embezzlement By Computer." *Security World,* September 1968, p. 26.

Allen, Brandt R. "Computer Fraud." *Financial Executive,* May 1971, pp. 38–44.

——. "Computer Security." *Data Management,* January 1971, p. 18.

——. "Danger Ahead! Safeguard Your Computer." *Harvard Business Review,* November–December 1968, pp. 97–101.

"Analyze Computer Use For Proper Protection." *Business Insurance,* July 1971, p. 34.

Armer, Paul. "Social Implications of the Computer Utility." *The Rand Corporation,* Santa Monica, Calif., August 1967.

"The Auditor Encounters Electronic Data Processing." *Price Waterhouse and Co.,* International Business Machines Corp., 1968.

Bates, William S. "Security of Computer-Based Information Systems." *Datamation,* May 1970, pp. 60–65.

Beardsley, Charles W. "Is Your Computer Insecure?" *Spectrum,* January 1972, p. 67.

Bigelow, R. P. "Some Legal Aspects of Commercial Remote Access Computer Services." *Datamation,* August 1969, pp. 48–52.

"Borden Net In Quarter, Half Fell From '67." *Wall Street Journal,* July 31, 1968, p. 10.

Boyer, Jerome T. "Fire Protection of Computers." *Industrial Security,* October 1971, p. 27.

"Business Spies Still Busy." *Industrial Management,* June 1969, pp. 58–59.

Byrns, T. "Considerations in Designing a Computer Communciations System." *Datamation,* October 1969, pp. 78–83.

Cadematori, Kenneth G. "The Impact of EDP On Auditing." *EDP and the Auditor,* Management Bulletin 81. New York: American Management Assn., 1966.

Carlson, Paul. "A Bank Protects Its 'Memory.'" *Banking,* April 1971, pp. 38–39.

Carr, Peter F. "Limiting Access To Centers Called A Major Problem." *Computerworld,* June 24, 1970, p. 1.

——. "Most DP Centers Lax In Arranging Backup Facilities." *Computerworld,* July 15, 1970, p. 1.

————. "Poor Security Leaves DP Facilities Ripe For Sabotage." *Computerworld*, June 17, 1970, p. 1.

Christiansen, Theodore W. "Data Processing Systems Controls." *Journal of Systems Management*, June 1969, pp. 8–10.

Chu, Albert L. C. "Computer's Achilles Heel." *Business Automation*, February 1, 1971, pp. 33–38.

————. "The Need To Know . . . The Right To Privacy." *Business Automation*, June 1, 1971, p. 24.

"Computer 'Capers' Herald New Crime Wave Of Embezzlement." *The National Underwriter*, August 20, 1971, p. 1.

"Computer Center Occupied For Bargaining Position." *Computerworld*, April 27, 1970, p. 1.

"Computer Communication Security." *Industrial Security*, June 1970, p. 24.

"Computer Con Men Are On the Rise," *Charlotte Observer*, August 16, 1970, p. 1.

"Computer Designs Tamperproof Computer." *Data Management*, September 1969, p. 55.

"Computer File Privacy In Great Britain." *The Office*, September 1971, pp. 41–44.

"Computer Fire Detection Systems." Manual of Prytronics, Inc. Cedar Knolls, N.J., 1970.

"Computer Security." Transcript of Panel of 15th Annual Seminar of American Society of Industrial Security, Washington, D.C., 1969. *Industrial Security*, December 1969, p. 18.

"Computer Security Is Sensitive Area." *Industry Week*, October 5, 1970, pp. 13–14.

"Computer Systems Security Has Received a Boost By the Introduction of a New Key Reader Assembly." *Security Systems Digest*, August 5, 1970, p. 4.

"Computer Tape: Cleanliness Counts." *Administrative Management*, May 1969, p. 32.

"Computers: How Do You Keep the Secrets Secret?" *Los Angeles Times*, November 23, 1971, p. 1.

"Computers Require Special Protection." Newark (N.J.) *Evening News*, May 19, 1970, p. 1.

"Considerations Of Data Security In a Computer Environment." *International Business Machines*, White Plains, N.Y.

"Controlling Government Computer Costs." *The Office*, July 1971, p. 28.

Cook, A. D. "EDP Defends Against Distaster." *Electronic News*, December 29, 1969, p. 33.

"Cryptic Computers." *Scientific American*, January 1970, p. 52.

"Cryptographic Package May End 360 Program Threats." *Computerworld*, June 24, 1970, p. 1.

Dansiger, S. "Dansiger Cites Ways To Ward Off Computer Embezzlement Problems." *Computerworld*, June 19, 1968, p. 4.

Darby, Edwin. "Fighting Computer Thieves." *Chicago Sun-Times*, June 24, 1970, p. 74.

Darling, Don. "Teleprinter, Printout Security." *Security World*, October 1970, p. 23.

"Data Processing Errors and Omissions Insurance." *Banking*, April 1971, pp. 38, 76.

"Data Processing Security." *Security Systems Digest*, July 8, 1970, p. 5.

Davidson, T. A. "Computer Information Privacy." *The Office*, August 1969, pp. 10–12.

Davis, Morton S. "Service Bureaus Need To Improve Data Security." *Computerworld*, August 26, 1970.

Diamond, T. D., and Krallinger, J. C. "Controls and Audit Trails For Real-Time Systems." *Internal Auditor*, November–December 1968.

Donovan, Robert D. "An Automated Document Declassification System. *Journal of the National Classification Management Society*, 1966, pp. 138–43.

Duggan, Michael A. "Software Protection." *Computerworld*, June 1969, p. 1.

"Electric Brownouts Add Unforeseen Risks For Company Using Computer." *Business Insurance*, September 13, 1971, p. 16.

"Electronic Computer/Data Processing Equipment." *National Fire Protection Association*, Boston, 1972.

"Electronic Security In the Computer Room." *Banking*, May 1970, p. 86.

"Employees Accused Of Illegal Computer Use." *Datamation*, December 1967, p. 78.

"Employees Now Pose Growing Security Risk." *Business Insurance*, July 5, 1971, pp. 37–38.

"Errors and Omissions Coverage Vital For Those Who Process Other's Data." *Business Insurance*, July 5, 1971, p. 38.

"Explosion Destroys H-22 At Phelps Dodge," *Datamation*, October 1966, p. 23.

Felsman, Robert A.; Chrisman, Thomas L.; Hope, Henry W.; Holder, John E.; and Medlock, V. Bryan Jr. "Computer Program Protection." *Texas Bar Journal*, January 1971, pp. 33, 40, 53–61.

"Firebombs Damage A Computer Center." *The Office*, August 1970, pp. 42–43.

Fitzpatrick, Robert J. "The Influence of EDP On Internal Control." *The Controller*, March 1961, p. 123.

Foster, C. C. "Data Banks: A Position Paper." *Computers and Automation*, March 1971, p. 28.

Freed, Roy. "Computer Fraud—A Management Trap." *Business Horizons*, June 1969, pp. 25–30.

Gellman, Harvey S. "Using The Computer To Steal." *Computers and Automation*, April 1971, pp. 16–18.

Godbout, William. "Computer Theft By Computer." *Security World*, May 1971, pp. 22–24.

Goodman, John V. "Auditing Magnetic Tape Systems." *The Computer Journal*, July 1964.

Grant, C. B. S. "Will Students Wreck Your Computer Center?" *Data Processing*, May 1969, pp. 62–63.

Greenberg, David. "Lawsuits Against Computer Firms." *Administrative Management*, April 1971, pp. 59–60.

Greenberg, Harold. "Privacy and Security." *Data Systems News*, August 1969, pp. 8–9.

"Ground Data Corporation Says It Is Now Marketing Two New Communications Systems Scramblers." *Security Systems Digest*, July 22, 1970, p. 7.

"Guard That Computer." *Nation's Business*, April 1971, pp. 84–86.

Gudie, A. H. "Are You Ready For EDP?" *The Electrical Distributor*, June 1971, p. 24.

"Guide For Auditing Automatic Data Processing Systems." *Department of the Air Force*, 1966.

Guise, R. F. "File Security." *Data Systems*, November 1969, p. 60.

"Halting the Electronic Hijacker." *Management Review*, November 1968, pp. 45–50.

Hanlon, Joseph. "Anti-War Protestors Erase 1,000 Dow Tapes." *Computerworld*, December 3, 1969, p. 1.

———. "Ten Students Convicted in 1969 Computer Center Burning." *Computerworld*, April 29, 1970, p. 1.

Hartnack, Carl E. "Internal and External Crimes Against Banks." *Security World*, September 1969, pp. 31–32.

"Heading Off An Energy Crisis." *Nation's Business*, July 1971, p. 26.

Healy, Richard J. "Disaster Planning." *Security World,* November 1965, p. 24.

Henderson, Robert P. "Record Keeping In the Space Age." Speech before National Symposium of the National Archives and Record Services (GSA), Washington, D.C., June 9, 1970.

Hoefler, Don. "The Hardware of Eavesdropping." *Security World,* May 1966, p. 18A.

"Housing Computers." *Administrative Management,* February 1971, pp. 34–35.

"How Bad Guys Thwart Computers." *The Office,* September 1970, pp. 36–39.

"How Paper Shredders Protect Business Data." *The Office,* September 1971, p. 58.

"How Security Does Pay Off." *The Office,* September 1971, pp. 22–26.

"How To Murder a Computer." *Chicago Seed,* 1970.

Howes, Paul R. "EDP Security: Is Your Guard Up?" *Management Review,* July 1971, pp. 29–32.

"Industry's Untold Multibillion-Dollar Story." *Nation's Business,* May 1971, p. 62.

"In-Office I-D Systems Aid Company Security." *Administrative Management,* April 1969, pp. 24–28.

"Inside Eastern's Data Center." *Business Week,* February 5, 1972, pp. 60–61.

"Insuring EDP Departments Against Disaster." *Supervisory Management,* September 1966, pp. 44–46.

Jacobson, Robert V. "Providing Security Protection For Computer Files." *Best's Review,* May 1970, pp. 42–44.

Johnson, Carl B. "Protection Primer For EDP Records." *Banking,* December 1969, pp. 85–86.

Johnson, J. E. "Engineering Early Warning Fire Detection." Printed privately, Cedar Knolls, N.J., 1969.

Keebler, Jim. "Speedy Computer People." *Automation,* May 1971, p. 39.

Koefod, Curtis F. "The Handling and Storage Of Computer Tape." *Data Processing,* July 1969, pp. 20–28.

Lang, William Jr. "Backup Files Are a Must." *Administrative Management,* October 1971, p. 55.

———. "Get It In Writing." *Administrative Management,* August 1971, p. 12.

Laver, Murray. "User's Influence On Computer Systems Design." *Datamation,* October 1969, pp. 107–18.

Levine, R. A. "How To Protect Your EDP Records."

New York Certified Public Accountant, May 1969, pp. 353–56.

Lutter, Frederick H. "Keeping the Computer Secure." *Administrative Management,* October 1970, pp. 10–14.

Miller, R. N. "Computers and the Law of Privacy." *Datamation,* September 1968, pp. 49–50.

Mintz, Harold K. "Safeguarding Computer Information." *Computers and Automation,* September 1969, p. 10.

Morran, J. Richard. "How Does Your Bank Stack Up In Insurance Against EDP Losses?" *Banking,* April 1970, pp. 36–37.

Morton, Thomas J. "Prevention of Public Access 'Key' To DP Center Security." *Computerworld,* June 9, 1971, p. 2.

"Most U.S. Companies Called Lax In Security Of Data Processing Centers." *Business Insurance,* June 22, 1970, p. 18.

Musolino, Anthony R. "Employee Security." *Industrial Security,* December 1970, pp. 32–34.

Nelson, F. Barry. "Campus Computers: Target For Militants and Almost Anyone Else." *Datamation,* October 15, 1970.

Neville, Haig G. "Letters To the Editor." *Harvard Business Review,* May–June 1969, pp. 40–42.

"New Threats and New Defenses." *Banking,* August 1970, pp. 69–70.

Nielsen, George E. "Computerized Access Controls." *Industrial Security,* October 1968, pp. 32–36.

Perham, J. "The Computer: A Target." *Dun's Review,* January 1971, p. 34.

Porter, Thomas W. "Evaluating Internal Controls in EDP Systems." *Journal of Accountancy,* August 1964, pp. 34–40.

Pratt, Lester A. "Embezzlement Controls For Business Enterprises." Private printing, March 1966.

"Privacy and Security." *Data Systems,* August 1969, p. 9.

"Problems and Potential Solution In Computer Control." *Industrial Security,* April 1969, pp. 34–50.

"Protecting Your Computer—Ask What It Does and What You Need To Backup." *Business Insurance,* July 5, 1971, pp. 31–32.

"Pushbutton Locks For Computer Room Security." *The Office*, March 1971, pp. 161–63.

Queeney, Jack. "Computer Spies: New Worry For Business." *Chicago's American*, January 16, 1969.

Reider, H. R. "Maintaining the Security Of Computer Records." *Burrough's Clearing House*, February 1971, p. 28.

Reynolds, J. H. "Computer Misuse: A Look At Vulnerable Areas." *Best's Review*, May 1971, p. 71.

Scaletta, Phillip J. "The Legal Ramifications Of the Computer Age." *Data Management*, November 1970, pp. 10–14.

Schiedermayer, Philip. "The Many Aspects Of Computer Security." *The Police Chief*, July 1970.

Scotese, Peter G. "What Top Management Expects of EDP." *Business Automation*, February 1, 1971, p. 48.

"Secured Cable Alarm Systems." *Mosler Safe Co. Bulletin*, 1970, p. 16.

"Security Defenses For the Computer Room." *Management Review*, May 1969, pp. 67–68.

"Security Men Thrive On the Wages of Fear." *Business Week*, June 20, 1970, pp. 112–14.

"Some Tips On Computer Security." *Industry Week*, August 3, 1970, p. 22.

Stubbs, James. "Filing and Finding Computer Tapes." *Administrative Management*, May 1969, p. 56.

Taylor, Robert L., and Feingold, Robert S. "Computer Data Protection." *Industrial Security*, August 1970, pp. 20–29.

"Technician Seized, Accused of Picking Computer's Brain." *Los Angeles Times*, March 3, 1971, p. 8.

"Telephones Used In Program Theft." *Business Automation*, April 1971, p. 7.

"Ten-Point Guide Offers EDP Security; Privacy." *Business Insurance*, July 5, 1971, pp. 31–32.

"Term Theft of Computer Data Sophisticated Crime." *Business Insurance*, June 9, 1969, p. 7.

Thorne, Jack F. "The Audit of Real Time Systems." *Data Management*, May 1970, p. 14.

———. "Internal Control of Real-Time Systems." *Data Management*, June 1970, pp. 34–37.

Toepfer, Edwin. "Lock Security." *Security World*, September 1965, p. 24.

"Twenty Students Take Over DP Center, Promise They

Don't Plan Any Damage." *Computerworld,* November 25, 1970, p. 1.

Twigg, Terry. "Need To Keep Digital Data Secure." *Electronic Design,* November 9, 1972, p. 68.

"$290,000 Awarded In Libel Damages To an Insurance Broker Suing Retail Credit Company." *Computers and Automation,* May 1971, p. 32.

Van Tassel, Dennis. "Keeping Confidential Information Confidential." *Systems Management,* February 1969, pp. 14–15.

―――. "Security In a Computer Environment." *Computers and Automation,* July 1969, pp. 24–26.

Verba, Joseph. "Protecting Your EDP Investment." *Management Services,* September–October 1970, pp. 37–40.

Wackenhut, George R. "Business Is the Target of Bombings and Bomb Hoaxes." *The Office,* September 1971, pp. 14–20.

Wasserman, J. J. "Plugging the Leaks In Computer Security." *Harvard Business Review,* September–October 1969, pp. 119–29.

―――. "Protecting Your Computer's Security." *Data Systems,* February 1970, p. 17.

Waterson, Lynn. "Data Banks Can Protect Privacy." *Banking,* January 1968, p. 56.

"Weapons and Ferromagnetic Objects Detected By a New Magnetic Searcher." *Computers and Automation,* January 1971, p. 51.

Wearstler, Earl W. "A Computer Center Is For Safety, Not For Show." *Banking,* April 1971, pp. 70–72.

Weiss, Harold. "The Dangers Of Total Corporate Amnesia." *Financial Executive,* June 1969, pp. 63–66.

Wessel, Milton R. "Computer Services and the Law." *Business Automation,* November 1970.

―――. "Legal Protection Of Computer Programs." *Harvard Business Review,* March–April 1965, pp. 97–105.

Worley, A. R. "Practical Aspects of Data Communication." *Datamation,* October 1969, pp. 60–66.

"Youth Convicted of Computer Fire." *Los Angeles Times,* February 10, 1971, p. 16.

Books

Auditing and EDP. New York: American Institute of Certified Public Accountants, 1968.

Brown, William F., ed. *Computer and Software Security.* New York: AMR International, 1972.

Greene, Richard M., Jr. *Business Intelligence and Espionage.* Homewood, Ill.: Dow Jones–Irwin, 1966.

Healy, Richard J. *Design For Security.* New York: John Wiley & Sons, 1968.

Hemphill, Charles F., Jr. *Security For Business and Industry.* Homewood, Ill.: Dow Jones–Irwin, 1971.

Kantner, J. *The Computer and the Executive.* New York: Prentice-Hall, 1967.

Kaufman, Felix. *Electronic Data Processing and Auditing.* New York: The Ronald Press Co., 1961.

Krauss, Leonard I. *Safe: Security Audit and Field Evaluation For Computer Facilities and Information Systems.* East Brunswick, N.J.: Firebrand, Krauss and Co., 1972.

Tryon, George H. *Fire Protection Handbook,* 13th ed. Cambridge, Mass.: Riverside Press, 1962.

Van Tassel, Dennis. *Computer Security Management.* New York: Prentice-Hall, 1972.

Westin, A. F. *Privacy and Freedom.* New York: Atheneum, 1967.

APPENDIX: SAMPLE
INSURANCE POLICIES

THE ST. PAUL
INSURANCE COMPANIES

Serving you around the world...around the clock

GENERAL INFORMATION
DATA PROCESSING POLICY

The Data Processing Policy has been designed to meet a real need to insure Electronic Data Processing Equipment and other machines related to the data processing operation on a broad "All Risks" basis. It is also designed to provide proper insurance on the very substantial exposure of Media as well as the Extra Expense involved to return to a normal operation after a loss to machines or media and the monetary loss due to Business Interruption.

The coverage is divided into four major sections, as follows:

Insuring Agreement No. 1. **DATA PROCESSING EQUIPMENT.** This portion insures all equipment and component parts related to the processing unit. A schedule must be obtained of the units to be covered, and it is optional whether all or part is to be insured. Many firms will rent much of the equipment, and in such cases, we are prepared to cover the Difference of Conditions to pick up the responsibility of the Insured. This, basically, would be perils over and above Fire and Extended Coverage. Valuation may be actual cash value or retail replacement cost. Coinsurance of 80%, 90%, and 100% on actual cash value is optional but 100% coinsurance is mandatory on replacement cost basis.

Insuring Agreement No. 2. **DATA PROCESSING MEDIA.** This section insures physical loss or damage to all forms of media and can include magnetic tapes, perforated paper tapes, punch cards, discs, drums, and other forms of communication related to the data processing unit—in other words, this media picks up the data after it is converted from the source material into a form which is used in the processing system. For example, in the insurance business, when the information from a policy copy is put on a punch card or magnetic tape or perforated tape, it is then in converted form. The daily report or copy of the policy is not covered in this example. The Insured may elect to insure all media or any specific part. Great care must be exercised in developing a risk to determine the proper valuation to be insured on media. We give the Insured the option of valuing on two bases. If they can establish and wish to set a fixed value on each item — for example, so much per reel of tape or so much per punch card — we will accept this valuation and it becomes valued. If no specific valuation is placed, then we pay the actual reproduction cost. Reproduction cost will mean what it would cost to replace the media after a loss. This cost, therefor, must be figured not only on the basis of what it cost to originally produce those records, but the additional expense that must be incurred as a result of a loss. This additional expense can be quite substantial because it may involve working at some other location or on an overtime basis. No coinsurance applies.

Insuring Agreement No. 3. **EXTRA EXPENSE.** This coverage is designed to insure the extra expense necessary to continue to conduct, as nearly as practicable, the normal operation of business, due to damage to or destruction of the processing system including equipment and component parts and the data processing media therefor. On the surface, this would appear to overlap Agreement No. 2, because it includes media. It was written this way to take care of situations where all media may not be insured, although it should be, and also in situations when the machines are damaged but there is no damage to the media. Here again, it is essential that great care be exercised in developing the proper exposure, not only for the protection of the Insured, but for rating the risk. It will be found that this extra expense item can be very substantial. No coinsurance applies.

Insuring Agreement No. 6. **BUSINESS INTERRUPTION.** This agreement designed for use with the Data Processing Policy to cover monetary loss resulting from total or partial suspension of operations by reason of direct physical loss to data processing equipment and active data processing media. Perils are all risk using a **valued** business interruption form.

Use of this Agreement, in combination with Extra Expense Insuring Agreement No. 3, rounds out the Insured's recovery program whenever extra expense, while compensating for extra expenses incurred, falls short in replacing production earnings lost when data processing equipment and media control daily production and when a definite loss to earnings can be demonstrated.

DEDUCTIBLES will be available in most states on Insuring Agreements Nos. 1, 2, 3 and 6 from $500 to $100,000 with appropriate credits. ($5,000 to $250,000 in New York)

(over)

14172 GID Rev. 9-66 Printed in U S A

228

VALUABLE PAPERS AND ACCOUNTS RECEIVABLE. These two parts tie into the general requirements of a firm and can be included in the contract. The Valuable Papers policy covers the source material plus any other valuable papers. It should be considered at the same time. Accounts Receivable is important since there may be a loss of receivables due to the destruction of the records.

INSPECTION. Each risk must be considered on its individual merits and a complete inspection will be necessary for each risk.

APPLICATION. The Application is designed to not only develop information for our own use, but to lead the Insured into a realization of his exposures and assist him in developing the proper amount of insurance. The Information Sheet should be used as a preliminary check of the exposures prior to inspection to determine the desirability of the risk.

RATES. Each risk will be rated individually, but the rates generally are based on the Fire, Extended Coverage, and Vandalism rate plus a loading to take care of the additional perils, plus any possible increase in the fire exposure not previously considered.

TERM. While it is preferable to write policies for only one year because of constant changes in valuations, exposures, equipment and procedures, policies can be written for a term of three years at the term multiple.

PROSPECTS. In addition to the obvious prospects such as insurance companies of all kinds, large manufacturers, banks and finance organizations, there are no doubt many other low hazard classes of risks that have small units of data processing equipment in various forms, which qualify, who also need this type of coverage.

THE ST. PAUL INSURANCE COMPANIES

Serving you around the world — around the clock

APPLICATION FOR DATA PROCESSING POLICY

PROPERTY DIVISION

NAME OF APPLICANT (INCLUDE NAMES OF ALL SUBSIDIARIES)

BUSINESS ADDRESS

NATURE OF BUSINESS	EFFECTIVE DATE	TERM

RATING INFORMATION

LOCATION 1						LOCATION 2					
CONTENTS FIRE RATE	COINS %	E. C. RATE	COINS. %	V. & M. M. RATE	COINS. %	CONTENTS FIRE RATE	COINS. %	E. C. RATE	COINS. %	V. & M. M. RATE	COINS. %

THE APPLICANT HAS THE OPTION of insuring only his data processing equipment, or his data processing media, or his extra expense or business interruption, or he may elect to take any two, three or four of the coverages. If desired, the applicant may also purchase these coverages on a deductible basis subject to a minimum deductible of $500.00.

DATA PROCESSING EQUIPMENT: The applicant has the option of insuring all or only part of the equipment, which may be either owned or leased, on an actual cash value basis or on a retail replacement cost basis.

ACTIVE DATA PROCESSING MEDIA: The applicant has the option of (1) specifically scheduling items or groups by types, establishing per-unit agreed values, or (2) blanketing all or unscheduled items into a total single value.

DATA PROCESSING EQUIPMENT

(Attach schedule or list below under "Additional Information")

LOCATION 1				LOCATION 2			
LIMIT OF LIABILITY	OWNED OR LEASED	ACTUAL CASH VALUE	REPLACEMENT COST	LIMIT OF LIABILITY	OWNED OR LEASED	ACTUAL CASH VALUE	REPLACEMENT COST
$		$	$	$		$	$

VALUATION		COINSURANCE			DEDUCTIBLE	
☐ ACTUAL CASH VALUE	☐ REPLACEMENT COST*	☐ 80%	☐ 90%	☐ 100%	☐ YES ☐ NO	$

*REPLACEMENT COST MUST BE WRITTEN WITH 100% COINSURANCE.

DATA PROCESSING MEDIA

LOCATION 1				LOCATION 2			
LIMIT OF LIABILITY	100% COINS. F.C. RATE	ACTUAL CASH VALUE	REPLACEMENT COST	LIMIT OF LIABILITY	100% COINS F.C. RATE	ACTUAL CASH VALUE	REPLACEMENT COST
$		$	$	$	$		$

LIMIT OF LIABILITY		DEDUCTIBLE	
$	WHILE IN TRANSIT AND WHILE TEMPORARILY WITHIN OTHER PREMISES.	☐ YES ☐ NO	$

EXTRA EXPENSE

AGREED "PERIOD OF RESTORATION"	ESTIMATED EXTRA EXPENSE TO BE INCURRED FOR THAT PERIOD	DEDUCTIBLE	
	$	☐ YES ☐ NO	$

BUSINESS INTERRUPTION

NUMBER OF "OPERATING DAYS" PER WEEK	AMOUNT OF INSURANCE	MEASURE OF RECOVERY PER DAY	DEDUCTIBLE	
	$	$	☐ YES ☐ NO	$

ADDITIONAL INFORMATION

14951 ADP REV. 12-64

230

MACHINE CHARACTERISTICS, OPERATION AND EXPOSURES

YES NO
- ☐☐ ARE ANY MACHINES ENCLOSED IN COMBUSTIBLE MATERIAL OR ARE PANELS LINED WITH COMBUSTIBLE INSULATION OR SOUND DEADENERS?
- ☐☐ IS THIS INSTALLATION IN A SPECIAL ROOM, HEREINAFTER REFERRED TO AS ''THE ROOM''?
- ☐☐ ARE COMPUTERS EQUIPPED WITH VACUUM TUBES?
- ☐☐ DOES ANY MACHINE CABLE OR WIRING OUTSIDE OF ROOM PASS THROUGH AREAS CONTAINING COMBUSTIBLE MATERIAL?
- ☐☐ ARE ALL UNITS INSIDE THE ROOM GOVERNED BY A MASTER SWITCH?
  - LOCATED: ☐ IN THE ROOM ☐ OUTSIDE THE ROOM
- ☐☐ ARE MANUFACTURER'S ENGINEERS PERMANENTLY ASSIGNED TO THE ROOM?
- ☐☐ IS THE ENGINEER'S WORKSHOP INSIDE THE ROOM?
- ☐☐ HAVE DEFINITE ARRANGEMENTS BEEN MADE FOR THE USE OF SUBSTITUTE FACILITIES ELSEWHERE IN THE EVENT OF A SHUTDOWN?

IS TAPE STORAGE (OTHER THAN TAPE IN USE):
- ☐ IN VAULT?
- ☐ IN COMPUTER ROOM?
- ☐ IN COMBUSTIBLE RACKS?
- ☐ IN APPROVED METAL CONTAINERS IN A 2-HOUR SAFE?

WHAT KIND OF TAPES ARE USED?
- ☐ METAL
- ☐ PLASTIC
- ☐ PAPER

YES NO
- ☐☐ IS FLAMMABLE SOLVENT USED FOR TAPE ROLLER OR CAPSTAN CLEANING?
- ☐☐ IS SOLVENT KEPT IN 6-OZ. CAN WITH SPOUT?
- ☐☐ IS FLAMMABLE SOLVENT KEPT IN GLASS BOTTLE?

AIR CONDITIONING EQUIPMENT

- ☐☐ IS ELECTRIC PRECIPITRON PROVIDED IN AIR STREAM TO ROOM?
- ☐☐ IS ROOM AIR CONDITIONED?
- ☐☐ ARE DUCT LININGS COMBUSTIBLE?
- ☐☐ ARE COMBUSTIBLE FILTERS USED?
- ☐☐ ARE FILTERS OIL-DIPPED?
- ☐☐ IS COMPRESSOR IN ROOM OR IMMEDIATELY ADJOINING?
- ☐☐ IS FREON USED AS REFRIGERANT?
- ☐☐ IS FRESH OR MAKE-UP AIR INTAKE:
- ☐☐ WITHIN 10 FT. OF THE GROUND?

- ☐☐ SCREENED WITH $\frac{1}{4}$ IN. OR HEAVIER GALVANIZED MESH?
- ☐☐ OVER ADJOINING BUILDINGS OR OVER ANY COMBUSTIBLE MATERIAL OR SUBJECT TO SMOKE FROM NEARBY (150 FT.) STACKS?
- ☐☐ DOES SYSTEM HAVE CONTROL SWITCH IN ROOM OR ELECTRIC EYE OR OTHER AUTOMATIC SHUTDOWN SWITCH?
- ☐☐ IS THERE ANY PROVISION FOR DUPLICATION IN EVENT OF SYSTEM SHUTDOWN?

WATER DAMAGE

- ☐☐ IS ROOM SUBJECT TO ACCUMULATION OF WATER FROM ITS OWN LEVEL?
- ☐☐ DO WATER LINES OTHER THAN SPRINKLER SYSTEM ENTER OR PASS THROUGH ROOM OR CEILING SPACE?
- ☐☐ DO STEAM LINES, OTHER THAN RADIATOR BRANCH LINES FOR COMPUTER ROOM, ENTER OR PASS THROUGH ROOM?

- ☐☐ ARE FLOOR(S) AND ROOF OVER ROOM WATER-TIGHT TO PREVENT ENTRY FROM ABOVE?
- ☐☐ ARE THERE SPRINKLERED AREAS OVER ROOM?
- ☐☐ IF ROOM IS SPRINKLERED, ARE COMPUTERS FITTED WITH IN- COMBUSTIBLE CANOPIES TO PREVENT ENTRY OF WATER FROM OVERHEAD?

COLLAPSE

- ☐☐ ARE THERE UNPROTECTED METAL SUPPORTS (POST OR BEAMS) ABOVE OR BELOW ROOM?

- ☐☐ ARE COMBUSTIBLE FLOORS ABOVE OR BELOW ROOM (EXCEL. PEDESTAL FLOOR)?
- ☐☐ ARE THERE SPRINKLERS ABOVE OR BELOW ROOM?

FIRE

- ☐☐ IS ROOM OF COMBUSTIBLE MATERIAL OR OF ANY MATERIAL ON COMBUSTIBLE STUDS OR SUPPORTS?
- ☐☐ IS ROOM NEAR OPEN COURTS OR STAIRWAYS OR IN VERTICAL FLUEWAY, OR RECEIVING OR DELIVERY DOCK OR PORT OR AD- JACENT TO PASSAGEWAY?
- ☐☐ DOES ROOM HAVE PEDESTAL FLOOR?
- ☐☐ IS PEDESTAL FLOOR OF COMBUSTIBLE MATERIAL?
- ☐☐ DOES ROOM CONTAIN COMBUSTIBLE CURTINS OR DRAPES?
- ☐☐ IS ROOM CEILING OF COMBUSTIBLE MATERIAL OR ON COMBUSTIBLE SUPPORTS?
- ☐☐ IS SMOKING PERMITTED IN ROOM OR IN ADJOINING REPAIR SHOP?
- ☐☐ DO WATCHMAN'S RECORDED ROUNDS TAKE HIM TO ROOM WHEN ROOM IS NOT OPERATING?
- ☐☐ ARE ADEQUATE CARBON DIOXIDE EXTINGUISHERS AVAILABLE IN ROOM?
- ☐☐ ARE GAS MASKS AVAILABLE FOR ROOM?

IS ANY REPAIR WORK DONE IN ROOM REQUIRING
- ☐ USE OF FLAME OR FLAMMABLE LIQUIDS
- ☐ STORAGE OF FLAMMABLE LIQUIDS
- ☐☐ IS THE ROOM EQUIPPED WITH SMOKE DETECTORS?
- ☐☐ ARE WINDOWS OF ROOM ON AN OUTSIDE WALL?

IF SO, DO THEY OVERLOOK OR FACE:
- ☐ A STREET WITHIN 15 FT. OF GROUND LEVEL?
- ☐ OTHER BUILDINGS, MATERIALS OR STRUCTURES?

EXPOSURE:
- ☐ NONE
- ☐ LIGHT
- ☐ MEDIUM
- ☐ SEVERE

DUPLICATE PROGRAM TAPES

- ☐☐ ARE DUPLICATE PROGRAM TAPES MAINTAINED?

- ☐☐ ARE THEY STORED IN FIREPROOF VAULT OR SAFE?
- ☐☐ ARE THEY STORED IN A BUILDING RATED AS A SEPARATE FIRE RISK?

AGENCY NAME, CITY AND STATE

ST. PAUL FIRE AND MARINE INSURANCE COMPANY

INSURANCE COMPANIES

Serving you around the world   around the clock

ST. PAUL FIRE AND MARINE INSURANCE COMPANY
(A Capital Stock Insurance Company, Herein Called the Company)

In consideration of the payment of premium, this Company does insure the Insured named in the Declarations subject to all of the terms and conditions of this Policy including all of the terms and conditions of the Declarations and Insuring Agreement(s) which are made a part thereof.

GENERAL POLICY CONDITIONS AND EXCLUSIONS

UNLESS PHYSICALLY DELETED BY THE COMPANY OR UNLESS SPECIFICALLY REFERRED TO IN THE INSURING AGREEMENT(S), THE FOLLOWING CLAUSES SHALL BE PARAMOUNT AND SHALL SUPERSEDE AND NULLIFY ANY CONTRARY PROVISIONS OF THE INSURING AGREEMENT(S).

1. GENERAL CONDITIONS

A. TERRITORIAL LIMITS: This Policy insures only while the property is at locations and while in transit within and between the forty-eight contiguous states of the United States of America, the District of Columbia and Canada, unless otherwise endorsed.

B. REMOVAL: Such insurance as is afforded by this Policy applies while the property insured is being removed to and while at place of safety because of imminent danger of loss, damage or expense and while being returned from such place, provided the Insured gives written notice to this Company of such removal within ten days thereafter.

C. OTHER INSURANCE: If there is available to the Insured or any other interested party any other insurance which would apply in the absence of this Policy, the insurance under this Policy shall apply only as excess insurance over such other insurance.

D. ASSIGNMENT: Assignment of interest under this Policy shall not bind the Company until its consent is endorsed hereon; if, however, the Insured shall die, or shall be adjudged bankrupt or insolvent and written notice is given to the Company within sixty days after the date of such adjudication, this Policy shall cover the Insured's legal representative as insured; provided that notice of cancelation addressed to the Insured named in this Policy and mailed to the address shown in this Policy shall be sufficient notice to effect cancelation of this Policy.

E. MISREPRESENTATION AND FRAUD: This Policy shall be void if the Insured has concealed or misrepresented any material fact or circumstance concerning this insurance or the subject thereof or in case of any fraud, attempted fraud or false swearing by the Insured touching any matter relating to this insurance or the subject thereof, whether before or after a loss.

F. NOTICE OF LOSS: The Insured shall as soon as practicable report to this Company or its agent every loss or damage which may become a claim under this Policy and shall also file with the Company or its agent within ninety (90) days from date of loss a detailed sworn proof of loss. Failure by the Insured to report the said loss or damage and to file such sworn proof of loss as hereinbefore provided shall invalidate any claim under this Policy for such loss.

ST. PAUL FIRE AND MARINE INSURANCE COMPANY
DATA PROCESSING POLICY

SPECIMEN

DECLARATIONS:

Name and address of Insured

A
G
E
N
T

FORMER POLICY NO.

The insurance afforded is only with respect to such and so many of the following Insuring Agreements as are indicated by ☒. The limit of this Company's liability shall be as stated herein, subject to all the terms of this Policy having reference thereto.

In states where required, the statutory fire conditions are made a part of this Policy.

POLICY PERIOD* FROM	TO	SUM INSURED	RATE	PREMIUM
		$		$

*AT NOON STANDARD TIME AT PLACE OF ISSUANCE AS TO EACH OF SAID DATES.

☐ **1. DATA PROCESSING SYSTEM EQUIPMENT:**

LIMITS OF LIABILITY (Paragraph 3)

A. On property of the Insured in the amount of:
   (1) $_____located at_____
   (2) $_____located at_____

B. On property leased, rented or under the control of the Insured in the amount of:
   (1) $_____located at_____
   (2) $_____located at_____

C. $_____while in transit and while temporarily within other premises.

VALUATION (Paragraph 6)		COINSURANCE CLAUSE (Paragraph 7)	DEDUCTIBLE (Paragraph 8)
☐ A. ACTUAL CASH VALUE CLAUSE	☐ B. REPLACEMENT COST CLAUSE	☐ A. ____% ☐ B. 100%	$

☐ **2. DATA PROCESSING MEDIA:**

LIMITS OF LIABILITY (Paragraph 3)

A. On property of the Insured in the amount of:
   (1) $_____located at_____
   (2) $_____located at_____

B. $_____while in transit and while temporarily within other premises.

VALUATION (Paragraph 6)	VALUE OF EACH	LIMITS OF INSURANCE
(A) Specified Articles	$	$
(B) All Others		
		$
		DEDUCTIBLE (Paragraph 7)
		$

☐ **3. EXTRA EXPENSE:** Subject of Insurance and Perils Insured (Paragraph 1):

AMOUNT OF INSURANCE	MEASURE OF RECOVERY (Paragraph 2)	DEDUCTIBLE (Paragraph 8)
$	$	$

COUNTERSIGNATURE DATE   COUNTERSIGNED AT   AGENT

14000 CAA Rev. 9-66 Printed in U. S. A.   (OVER)

234

☐ 4. VALUABLE PAPERS AND RECORDS

PROPERTY COVERED (Paragraph 1)

	VALUE OF EACH	LIMITS OF INSURANCE
A. Specified Articles	$	$
B. All Others		$

LOCATION AND OCCUPANCY OF PREMISES

PART OF BUILDING INSURED OCCUPIES	LOCATION OF BUILDING	BUSINESS INSURED CONDUCTS THEREIN

PROTECTION OF VALUABLE PAPERS AND RECORDS (Paragraph 4)

KIND OF RECEPTACLE	NAME OF MAKER	"CLASS" OR "HOUR EXPOSURE" OF LABEL	NAME OF ISSUER OF LABEL

☐ 5. ACCOUNTS RECEIVABLE

LOCATION AND OCCUPANCY OF PREMISES (Paragraph 4)

PART OF BUILDING INSURED OCCUPIES	LOCATION OF BUILDING	BUSINESS INSURED CONDUCTS THEREIN

PROTECTION OF RECORDS OF ACCOUNTS RECEIVABLE (Paragraph 4)

KIND OF RECEPTACLE	NAME OF MAKER	"CLASS" OR "HOUR EXPOSURE" OF LABEL	NAME OF ISSUER OF LABEL

LIMIT OF INSURANCE (Paragraph 5)	PROVISIONAL PREMIUM (Paragraph 2 of "Special Conditions")	
$	$	INCLUDED

☐ 6. BUSINESS INTERRUPTION: Subject of Insurance and Perils Insured (Paragraph 1)

AMOUNT OF INSURANCE	MEASURE OF RECOVERY (Paragraph 2)	DEDUCTIBLE (Paragraph 8)
$	$ PER DAY	$

235

This Policy is not complete unless
a Declarations Page is attached.

G. SETTLEMENT OF LOSS: All adjusted claims shall be paid or made good to the Insured within thirty days after presentation and acceptance of satisfactory proofs of interest and loss at the office of this Company. No loss shall be paid or made good if the Insured has collected the same from others.

H. SUE & LABOR: In case of loss or damage, it shall be lawful and necessary for the Insured, or his or their factors, servants and assigns, to sue, labor and travel for, in and about the defense, safeguard and recovery of the property insured hereunder, or any part thereof, without prejudice to this insurance; nor shall the acts of the Insured or this Company, in recovering, saving and preserving the property insured in case of loss or damage, be considered a waiver or an acceptance of abandonment, to the charge whereof this Company will contribute according to the rate and quantity of the sum herein insured.

I. SUIT: No suit, action or proceeding for the recovery of any claim under this Policy shall be sustainable in any court of law or equity unless the same be commenced within twelve (12) months next after discovery by the Insured of the occurrence which gives rise to the claim. Provided, however, that if by the laws of the State within which this Policy is issued such limitation is invalid, then any such claims shall be void unless such action, suit or proceeding be commenced within the shortest limit of time permitted by the laws of such State.

J. SUBROGATION: In the event of any payment under this Policy the Company shall be subrogated to all the Insured's rights of recovery therefor against any person or organization and the Insured shall execute and deliver instruments and papers and do whatever else is necessary to secure such rights. The Insured shall do nothing after loss to prejudice such rights.

K. APPRAISAL: If the Insured and the Company fail to agree as to the amount of loss, each shall, on the written demand of either, made within sixty (60) days after receipt of proof of loss by the Company, select a competent and disinterested appraiser, and the appraisal shall be made at a reasonable time and place. The appraisers shall first select a competent and disinterested umpire, and failing for fifteen days to agree upon such umpire, then, on the request of the Insured or the Company, such umpire shall be selected by a judge of a court of record in the county and state in which such appraisal is pending. The appraisers shall then appraise the loss, and failing to agree shall submit their differences to the umpire. An award in writing of any two shall determine the amount of loss. The Insured and the Company shall each pay its chosen appraiser and shall bear equally the expenses of the umpire and the other expenses of appraisal. The Company shall not be held to have waived any of its rights by any act relating to appraisal.

L. EXAMINATION UNDER OATH: The Insured shall submit, and so far as is within his or their power shall cause all other persons interested in the property and employees to submit, to examinations under oath by any persons named by the Company, relative to any and all matters in connection with a claim and subscribe the same; and shall produce for examination all books of account, bills, invoices, and other vouchers or certified copies thereof if originals be lost, at such reasonable time and place as may be designated by the Company or its representatives, and shall permit extracts and copies thereof to be made.

M. AUTOMATIC REINSTATEMENT: Any loss hereunder shall not reduce the amount of the Policy.

N. DEBRIS REMOVAL: This Policy is extended to cover expenses incurred in the removal of all debris of the damaged property insured hereunder which may be occasioned by loss caused by any of the perils insured against in this Policy. In no event shall the additional coverage granted by this paragraph increase the Limit of Liability specified in the "Declarations".

O. CANCELATION: This Policy may be canceled by the Insured by mailing to the Company written notice stating when thereafter such cancelation shall be effective. This Policy may be canceled by the Company by mailing to the Insured at the address shown in this Policy written notice stating when not less than ten (10) days thereafter such cancelation shall be effective. The mailing of notice as aforesaid shall be sufficient proof of notice and the effective date of cancelation stated in the notice shall become the end of the policy period. Delivery of such written notice either by the Insured or by the Company shall be equivalent to mailing.

If the Insured cancels, earned premiums shall be computed in accordance with the customary short rate table and procedure. If the Company cancels, earned premiums shall be computed pro rata. Premium adjustment may be made at the time cancelation is effected and, if not then made, shall be made as soon as practicable after cancelation becomes effective. The Company's check or the check of its representative mailed or delivered as aforesaid shall be a sufficient tender of any refund of premium due to the Insured.

P. CONFORMITY TO STATUTE: Terms of this Policy which are in conflict with the statutes of the State wherein this Policy is issued are hereby amended to conform to such statutes.

2. **PERILS EXCLUDED:** This Policy does not insure against loss, damage or expense caused directly or indirectly by:

A. (1) Hostile or warlike action in time of peace or war, including action in hindering, combating or defending against an actual impending or expected attack, (a) by any government or sovereign power (de jure or de facto), or by any authority maintaining or using military, naval or air forces; or (b) by military, naval or air forces; or (c) by an agent of any such government, power, authority or forces;

(2) Any weapon of war employing atomic fission or radioactive force whether in time of peace or war;

(3) Insurrection, rebellion, revolution, civil war, usurped power, or action taken by governmental authority in hindering, combating or defending against such an occurrence, seizure or destruction under quarantine or Customs regulations, confiscation by order of any government or public authority, or risks of contraband or illegal transportation or trade;

B. Nuclear reaction or nuclear radiation or radioactive contamination, all whether controlled or uncontrolled, and whether such loss be direct or indirect, proximate or remote, or be in whole or in part caused by, contributed to, or aggravated by the peril(s) insured against in this Policy; however, subject to the foregoing and all provisions of this Policy, direct loss by fire resulting from nuclear reaction or nuclear radiation or radioactive contamination is insured against by this Policy.

THIS POLICY IS MADE AND ACCEPTED SUBJECT TO THE FOREGOING STIPULATIONS AND CONDITIONS, together with such other provisions, agreements or conditions as may be endorsed hereon or added hereto; and no officer, agent or other representative of this Company shall have power to waive or be deemed to have waived any provision or condition of this Policy unless such waiver, if any, shall be written upon or attached hereto, nor shall any privilege or permission affecting the insurance under this Policy exist or be claimed by the Insured unless so written or attached.

PROVISIONS REQUIRED BY LAW TO BE STATED IN THIS POLICY:—"This Policy is issued under and in pursuance of the laws of the State of Minnesota, relating to Guaranty Surplus and Special Reserve Funds." Chapter 437, General Laws of 1909.

IN WITNESS WHEREOF, this Company has executed and attested these presents; but this Policy shall not be valid unless countersigned on the Declarations Page by a duly authorized Agent of the Company.

Secretary.

President.

14000 MPP   Rev. 11-65

INSURING AGREEMENT No. 1

Data Processing System Equipment

1. **PROPERTY COVERED:** Data processing systems including equipment and component parts thereof owned by the Insured or leased, rented or under the control of the Insured, all as per schedule(s) on file with this Company.

2. **PROPERTY EXCLUDED:** This Insuring Agreement does not insure:
   A. Active data processing media which is hereby defined as meaning all forms of converted data and/or program and/or instruction vehicles employed in the Insured's data processing operation;
   B. Accounts, bills, evidences of debt, valuable papers, records, abstracts, deeds, manuscripts, or other documents;
   C. Property rented or leased to others while away from the premises of the Insured.

3. **LIMITS OF LIABILITY:** See "DECLARATIONS".

4. **PERILS INSURED:** This Insuring Agreement insures against all risks of direct physical loss or damage to the property covered, except as hereinafter provided.

5. **PERILS EXCLUDED:** This Insuring Agreement does not insure against loss, damage or expense caused directly or indirectly by:
   A. Damage due to mechanical failure, faulty construction, error in design unless fire or explosion ensues, and then only for loss, damage, or expense caused by such ensuing fire or explosion;
   B. Inherent vice, wear, tear, gradual deterioration or depreciation;
   C. Any dishonest, fraudulent or criminal act by any Insured, a partner therein or an officer, director or trustee thereof, whether acting alone or in collusion with others;
   D. Dryness or dampness of atmosphere, extremes of temperature, corrosion, or rust unless directly resulting from physical damage to the data processing system's air conditioning facilities caused by a peril not excluded by the provisions of this Insuring Agreement;
   E. Short circuit, blow-out, or other electrical disturbance, other than lightning, within electrical apparatus, unless fire or explosion ensues and then only for loss, damage or expense caused by such ensuing fire or explosion;
   F. Actual work upon the property covered, unless fire or explosion ensues, and then only for loss, damage, or expense caused by such ensuing fire or explosion;
   G. Delay or loss of market;
   H. War risks or nuclear risks as excluded in the Policy to which this Insuring Agreement is attached.

6. **VALUATION:**
   A. ACTUAL CASH VALUE — The following clause shall apply if indicated in the "Declarations": This Company shall not be liable beyond the actual cash value of the property at the time any loss or damage occurs and the loss or damage shall be ascertained according to such actual value with proper deduction for depreciation, however caused, and shall in no event exceed what it would then cost to repair or replace the same with material of like kind and quality.
   B. REPLACEMENT COST — The following clause shall apply if indicated in the "Declarations": This Company shall not be liable beyond the actual retail replacement cost of the property at the time any loss or damage occurs and the loss or damage shall be ascertained or estimated on the basis of the actual cash retail replacement cost of property similar in kind to that insured at the place of and immediately preceding the time of such loss or damage, but in no event to exceed the limit of liability stipulated in the "Declarations".

7. **COINSURANCE CLAUSE:**
   A. The following clause shall apply if indicated in the "Declarations": This Company shall be liable in the event of loss for no greater proportion thereof than the amount hereby insured bears to the percent indicated in the "Declarations" of the actual cash value of all property insured hereunder at the time such loss shall happen.
   B. The following clause shall apply if indicated in the "Declarations": This Company shall be liable in the event of loss for no greater proportion thereof than the amount hereby insured bears to the percent indicated in the "Declarations" of the actual cash retail replacement cost of all property insured hereunder at the time such loss shall happen.

8. **DEDUCTIBLE:** Each and every loss occurring hereunder shall be adjusted separately and from the amount of each such loss when so adjusted the amount indicated in the "Declarations" shall be deducted.

9. **DIFFERENCE IN CONDITIONS:** It is a condition of this Insurance that the Insured shall file with this Company a copy of any lease or rental agreement pertaining to the property insured hereunder insofar as concerns the lessors' liability for loss or damage to said property, and coverage afforded hereunder shall be only for the difference in conditions between those contained in said lease or rental agreement and the terms of this Insuring Agreement. The Insured agrees to give this Company thirty days notice of any alteration, cancellation or termination of the above mentioned lease or rental agreement pertaining to the lessors' liability.

All other terms and conditions of the Policy not in conflict herewith remain unchanged.

14000 CAC 5-69 4M Rev. 12-64 Printed in U. S. A.

INSURING AGREEMENT No. 2
Data Processing Media

1. **PROPERTY INSURED:** Active data processing media, being property of the Insured or property of others for which the Insured may be liable.

2. **PROPERTY EXCLUDED:** This Insuring Agreement does not insure accounts, bills, evidences of debt, valuable papers, records, abstracts, deeds, manuscripts or other documents except as they may be converted to data processing media form, and then only in that form, or any data processing media which cannot be replaced with other of like kind and quality.

3. **LIMITS OF LIABILITY:** See "DECLARATIONS".

4. **PERILS INSURED:** This Insuring Agreement insures against all risks of direct physical loss or damage to the property covered, except as hereinafter provided.

5. **PERILS EXCLUDED:** This Insuring Agreement does not insure against loss, damage, or expense resulting from or caused directly or indirectly by:

   A. Data processing media failure or breakdown or malfunction of the data processing system including equipment and component parts while said media is being run through the system, unless fire or explosion ensues and then only for the loss, damage or expense caused by such ensuing fire or explosion;

   B. Electrical or magnetic injury, disturbance or erasure of electronic recordings, except by lightning;

   C. Dryness or dampness of atmosphere, extremes of temperature, corrosion, or rust unless directly resulting from physical damage to the data processing system's air conditioning facilities caused by a peril not excluded by the provisions of this Insuring Agreement;

   D. Delay or loss of market;

   E. Inherent vice, wear, tear, gradual deterioration or depreciation;

   F. Any dishonest, fraudulent or criminal act by any Insured, a partner therein or an officer, director or trustee thereof, whether acting alone or in collusion with others;

   G. War risks or nuclear risks as excluded in the Policy to which this Insuring Agreement is attached.

6. **VALUATION:** The limit of this Company's liability for loss or damage shall not exceed:

   A. As respects property specifically described in the "Declarations", the amount per article specified therein, said amount being the agreed value thereof for the purpose of this insurance;

   B. As respects all other property, the actual reproduction cost of the property; if not replaced or reproduced, blank value of media; all subject to the applicable limit of liability stated in the "Declarations".

7. **DEDUCTIBLE:** Each and every loss occurring hereunder shall be adjusted separately and from the amount of each loss when so adjusted the amount indicated in the "Declarations" shall be deducted.

8. **DEFINITIONS:** The term "active data processing media", wherever used in this contract, shall mean all forms of converted data and/or program and/or instruction vehicles employed in the Insured's data processing operation, except all such UNUSED property, and the following

_____
(insert names of media not to be insured)

which the Insured elects not to insure hereunder.

All other terms and conditions of the Policy not in conflict herewith remain unchanged.

14000 **CAD** Rev. 3-63

INSURING AGREEMENT No. 3
Extra Expense

1. **SUBJECT OF INSURANCE AND PERILS INSURED:** This Insuring Agreement insures against the necessary Extra Expense, as hereinafter defined, incurred by the Insured in order to continue as nearly as practicable the normal operation of its business, immediately following damage to or destruction of the data processing system including equipment and component parts thereof and data processing media therefor, owned, leased, rented or under the control of the Insured, as a direct result of all risks of physical loss or damage, but in no event to exceed the amount indicated in the "Declarations".

   This Insuring Agreement is extended to include actual loss as covered hereunder, sustained during the period of time, hereinafter defined, (1) when as a direct result of a peril insured against the premises in which the property is located is so damaged as to prevent access to such property or (2) when as a direct result of a peril insured against, the air conditioning system or electrical system necessary for the operation of the data processing equipment is so damaged as to reduce or suspend the Insured's ability to actually perform the operations normally performed by the data processing system.

2. **MEASURE OF RECOVERY:** If the above described property is destroyed or so damaged by the perils insured against occurring during the term of this Insuring Agreement so as to necessitate the incurrence of Extra Expense (as defined in this Insuring Agreement), this Company shall be liable for the Extra Expense so incurred, not exceeding the actual loss sustained, for not exceeding such length of time, hereinafter referred to as the "period of restoration", commencing with the date of damage or destruction and not limited by the date of expiration of this Insuring Agreement, as shall be required with the exercise of due diligence and dispatch to repair, rebuild, or replace such part of said property as may be destroyed or damaged.

   This Company's liability, during the determined period of restoration, shall be limited to the declared amount per period of time indicated in the "Declarations" but in no event to exceed the amount of insurance provided.

3. **EXTRA EXPENSE DEFINITION:** The term "Extra Expense" wherever employed in this Insuring Agreement is defined as the excess (if any) of the total cost during the period of restoration of the operation of the business over and above the total cost of such operation that would normally have been incurred during the same period had no loss occurred; the cost in each case to include expense of using other property or facilities of other concerns or other necessary emergency expenses. In no event, however, shall this Company be liable for loss of profits or earnings resulting from diminution of business, nor for any direct or indirect property damage loss insurable under Property Damage policies, or for expenditures incurred in the purchase, construction, repair or replacement of any physical property unless incurred for the purpose of reducing any loss under this Insuring Agreement not exceeding, however, the amount in which the loss is so reduced. Any salvage value of property so acquired which may be sold or utilized by the Insured upon resumption of normal operations, shall be taken into consideration in the adjustment of any loss hereunder.

4. **EXCLUSIONS:** It is a condition of the insurance that the Company shall not be liable for Extra Expense incurred as a result of:

   A. Any local or State ordinance or law regulating construction or repair of buildings;

   B. The suspension, lapse or cancellation of any lease, license, contract or order;

   C. Interference at premises by strikers or other persons with repairing or replacing the property damaged or destroyed or with the resumption or continuation of the Insured's occupancy;

   D. Loss or destruction of accounts, bills, evidences of debt, valuable papers, records, abstracts, deeds, manuscripts or other documents except as they may be converted to data processing media form and then only in that form;

   E. Loss of or damage to property rented or leased to others while away from the premises of the Insured;

   F. Error in machine programming or instructions to machine;

   G. Inherent vice, wear, tear, gradual deterioration or depreciation;

   H. Any dishonest, fraudulent or criminal act by any Insured, a partner therein or an officer, director or trustee thereof, whether acting alone or in collusion with others;

   I. Damage due to mechanical failure, faulty construction, error in design unless fire or explosion ensues, and then only for loss, damage, or expense caused by such ensuing fire or explosion;

   J. Short circuit, blow-out, or other electrical disturbance, other than lightning, within electrical apparatus, unless fire or explosion ensues and then only for loss, damage or expense caused by such ensuing fire or explosion;

   K. Delay or loss of market;

   L. War risks or nuclear risks as excluded in the Policy to which this Insuring Agreement is attached.

11000 CAV Rev 1-64 Printed in U. S. A.   (over)

240

5. **RESUMPTION OF OPERATIONS:** As soon as practicable after any loss, the Insured shall resume complete or partial business operations of the property herein described and, in so far as practicable, reduce or dispense with such additional charges and expenses as are being incurred.

6. **INTERRUPTION BY CIVIL AUTHORITY:** This Insuring Agreement is extended to include the actual loss sustained by the Insured, resulting directly from an interruption of business as covered hereunder, during the length of time, not exceeding 2 consecutive weeks, when, as a direct result of damage to or destruction of property adjacent to the premises herein described by the peril(s) insured against, access to such described premises is specifically prohibited by order of civil authority.

7. **DEFINITIONS:** The term "Normal" wherever used in this contract shall mean: The condition that would have existed had no loss occurred.

8. **DEDUCTIBLE:** Each and every loss occurring hereunder shall be adjusted separately and from the amount of each such loss when so adjusted the amount indicated in the "Declarations" shall be deducted.

All other terms and conditions of the Policy not in conflict herewith remain unchanged.

INSURING AGREEMENT No. 4
Valuable Papers and Records

1. **PROPERTY COVERED:** The Company agrees to pay on valuable papers and records, as stated in the "Declarations".

2. **THIS INSURING AGREEMENT INSURES AGAINST:** All risks of direct physical loss of or damage to the property covered, except as hereinafter provided, occurring during the period of this Insuring Agreement.

3. **LOCATION AND OCCUPANCY OF PREMISES:** See "DECLARATIONS".

4. **PROTECTION OF VALUABLE PAPERS AND RECORDS:** Insurance under this Insuring Agreement shall apply only while valuable papers and records are contained in the premises described in the "Declarations", it being a condition precedent to any right of recovery hereunder that such valuable papers and records shall be kept in the receptacle(s) described in the "Declarations" at all times when the premises are not open for business, except while such valuable papers and records are in actual use or as stated in paragraph 5 of this Insuring Agreement and 1B of Policy General Conditions.

5. **AUTOMATIC EXTENSION:** Such insurance as is afforded by this Insuring Agreement applies while the valuable papers and records are being conveyed outside the premises and while temporarily within other premises, except for storage, provided the Company's liability for such loss or damage shall not exceed ten percent of the combined limits of insurance stated in paragraph 1, nor Five Thousand Dollars, whichever is less.

EXCLUSIONS
THIS INSURING AGREEMENT DOES NOT APPLY:

(a) to loss due to wear and tear, gradual deterioration, vermin or inherent vice;

(b) to loss due to any fraudulent, dishonest, or criminal act by any Insured, a partner therein, or an officer, director or trustee thereof, whether acting alone or in collusion with others;

(c) to loss to property not specifically declared and described in section (a) of paragraph 1, "Property Covered", if such property cannot be replaced with other of like kind and quality;

(d) to loss to property held as samples or for sale or for delivery after sale;

(e) to loss due to electrical or magnetic injury, disturbance or erasure of electronic recordings, except by lightning;

(f) to war risks or nuclear risks as excluded in the Policy to which this Insuring Agreement is attached;

(g) to loss directly resulting from errors or omissions in processing or copying unless fire or explosion ensues and then only for direct loss caused by such ensuing fire or explosion.

SPECIAL CONDITIONS

1. **OWNERSHIP OF PROPERTY; INTERESTS COVERED:** The insured property may be owned by the Insured or held by him in any capacity; provided, the insurance applies only to the interest of the Insured in such property, including the Insured's liability to others, and does not apply to the interest of any other person or organization in any of said property unless included in the Insured's proof of loss.

2. **LIMITS OF LIABILITY; VALUATION; SETTLEMENT OPTION:** The limit of the Company's liability for loss shall not exceed the actual cash value of the property at time of loss nor what it would then cost to repair or replace the property with other of like kind and quality, nor the applicable limit of insurance stated in this Insuring Agreement; provided, as respects property specifically described in section (a) of paragraph 1, "Property Covered", the amount per article specified therein is the agreed value thereof for the purpose of this insurance. The Company may pay for the loss in money or may repair or replace the property and may settle any claim for loss of the property either with the Insured or the owner thereof. Any property so paid for or replaced shall become the property of the Company. The Insured or the Company, upon recovery of any such property, shall give notice thereof as soon as practicable to the other and the Insured shall be entitled to the property upon reimbursing the Company for the amount so paid or the cost of replacement.

   Application of the insurance to property of more than one person shall not operate to increase the applicable limit of insurance.

3. **INSURED'S DUTIES WHEN LOSS OCCURS:** Upon knowledge of loss or of an occurrence which may give rise to a claim for loss, the Insured shall give notice thereof as soon as practicable to the Company or any of its authorized agents and, if the loss is due to a violation of law, also to the police.

4. **ACTION AGAINST COMPANY:** No action shall lie against the Company unless, as a condition precedent thereto, there shall have been full compliance with all the terms of this Insuring Agreement, nor until thirty days after the required proofs of loss have been filed with the Company, nor at all unless commenced within two years after the discovery by the Insured of the occurrence which gives rise to the loss. If this limitation of time is shorter than that prescribed by any statute controlling the construction of this Insuring Agreement, the shortest permissible statutory limitation in time shall govern and shall supersede the time limitation herein stated.

5. **DEFINITIONS:**

   (a) Valuable Papers and Records — The term "valuable papers and records" means written, printed or otherwise inscribed documents and records, including books, maps, films, drawings, abstracts, deeds, mortgages and manuscripts, but does not mean money or securities, or electronic data control tapes.

   (b) Premises — The unqualified word "premises" means the interior of that portion of the building at the location designated in paragraph 3, "Location and Occupancy of Premises" and described in the "Declarations", which is occupied by the Insured for the business purposes stated therein.

6. **CHANGES:** Notice to any agent or knowledge possessed by any agent or by any other person shall not effect a waiver or a change in any part of this Insuring Agreement or estop the Company from asserting any right under the terms of this Insuring Agreement nor shall the terms of this Insuring Agreement be waived or changed, except by endorsement issued to form a part of this Insuring Agreement.

INAPPLICABLE POLICY CONDITIONS

Paragraph 1A, 1F, 1G, 1H, 1I and 1N of General Policy Conditions do not apply to this Insuring Agreement.

All other terms and conditions of the Policy not in conflict herewith remain unchanged.

14000 CAF Rev. 6-65

Accounts Receivable

1. **THE COMPANY AGREES TO PAY:**

   A. All sums due the Insured from customers, provided the Insured is unable to effect collection thereof as the direct result of loss of or damage to records of accounts receivable;

   B. Interest charges on any loan to offset impaired collections pending repayment of such sums made uncollectible by such loss or damage;

   C. Collection expense in excess of normal collection cost and made necessary because of such loss or damage;

   D. Other expenses, when reasonably incurred by the Insured in re-establishing records of accounts receivable following such loss or damage.

2. **THIS INSURING AGREEMENT INSURES AGAINST:** All risks of loss of or damage to the Insured's records of accounts receivable, occurring during the period of this Insuring Agreement, except as hereinafter provided.

3. **LOCATION AND OCCUPANCY OF PREMISES:** See "DECLARATIONS".

4. **PROTECTION OF RECORDS OF ACCOUNTS RECEIVABLE:** Insurance under this Insuring Agreement shall apply only while records of accounts receivable are contained in the premises described in the "Declarations", it being a condition precedent to any right of recovery hereunder that such records shall be kept in the receptacle(s) described in the "Declarations" at all times when the premises are not open for business, except while such records are in actual use;

5. **LIMIT OF INSURANCE:** The Company shall not be liable hereunder for an amount to exceed the Limit of Insurance stated in the "Declarations".

EXCLUSIONS

THIS INSURING AGREEMENT DOES NOT APPLY:

(a) to loss due to any fraudulent, dishonest or criminal act by any Insured, a partner therein, or an officer, director or trustee thereof, while working or otherwise and whether acting alone or in collusion with others;

(b) to loss due to bookkeeping, accounting or billing errors or omissions;

(c) to loss, the proof of which as to factual existence, is dependent upon an audit of records or an inventory computation; but this shall not preclude the use of such procedures in support of claim for loss which the Insured can prove, through evidence wholly apart therefrom, is due solely to a risk of loss to records of accounts receivable not otherwise excluded hereunder;

(d) to loss due to alteration, falsification, manipulation, concealment, destruction or disposal of records of accounts receivable committed to conceal the wrongful giving, taking, obtaining or withholding of money, securities or other property but only to the extent of such wrongful giving, taking, obtaining or withholding;

(e) to loss due to electrical or magnetic injury, disturbance or erasure of electronic recordings, except by lightning;

(f) to war risks or nuclear risks as excluded in the Policy to which this Insuring Agreement is attached.

SPECIAL CONDITIONS

1. **DEFINITION OF PREMISES:** The unqualified word "premises" means the interior of that portion of the building at the location designated in Paragraph 3, "location and occupancy of premises" and described in the "Declarations", which is occupied by the Insured for the business purposes stated therein.

2. **PREMIUM:** The Insured shall, within twenty days after the end of each fiscal month during the policy period, furnish the Company with a written statement of the total amount of accounts receivable, with deferred payments and charge accounts segregated, as of the last day of each such month.

   The premium stated in the "Declarations" is provisional only. Upon each anniversary and upon termination of this Insuring Agreement, the sum of the monthly amounts of accounts receivable for the preceding twelve months shall be averaged and the earned premium shall be computed on such average at the rate stated in this Insuring Agreement, whether or not such average exceeds the applicable limit of Insurance under this Insuring Agreement. If the earned premium thus computed exceeds the provisional premium paid, the Insured shall pay the excess to the Company; if less, the Company shall return to the Insured the unearned portion paid by the Insured, but such premium shall not be less than any minimum premium stated in this Insuring Agreement.

3. **INSPECTION AND AUDIT:** The Company shall be permitted to inspect the premises and the receptacles in which the records of accounts receivable are kept by the Insured, and to examine and audit the Insured's books and records at any time during the period of coverage and any extension thereof and within three years after the final termination of this Insuring Agreement, as far as they relate to the premium basis or the subject matter of this insurance, and to verify the statements of any outstanding record of accounts receivable submitted by the Insured and the amount of recoveries of accounts receivable on which the Company has made any settlement.

4. **RECOVERIES:** After payment of loss all amounts recovered by the Insured on accounts receivable for which the Insured has been indemnified shall belong and be paid to the Company by the Insured up to the total amount of loss paid by the Company; but all recoveries in excess of such amounts shall belong to the Insured.

5. **INSURED'S DUTIES WHEN LOSS OCCURS:** Upon the occurrence of any loss which may result in a claim hereunder, the Insured shall:

   (A) Give notice thereof as soon as practicable to the Company or any of its authorized agents and, if the loss is due to a violation of law, also to the police;

   (B) File detailed proof of loss, duly sworn to, with the Company promptly on expiration of ninety days from the date on which the records of accounts receivable were lost or damaged.

   Upon the Company's request, the Insured shall submit to examination by the Company, subscribe the same, under oath if required, and produce for the Company's examination all pertinent records, all at such reasonable times and places as the Company shall designate, and shall cooperate with the Company in all matters pertaining to loss or claims with respect thereto, including rendering of all possible assistance to effect collection of outstanding accounts receivable.

6. **DETERMINATION OF RECEIVABLES: DEDUCTIONS** — When there is proof that a loss covered by this Insuring Agreement has occurred but the Insured cannot accurately establish the total amount of accounts receivable outstanding as of the date of such loss, such amount shall be based on the Insured's monthly statements and shall be computed as follows:

   (a) determine the amount of all outstanding accounts receivable at the end of the same fiscal month in the year immediately preceding the year in which the loss occurs;

   (b) calculate the percentage of increase or decrease in the average monthly total of accounts receivable for the twelve months immediately preceding the month in which the loss occurs, or such part thereof for which the Insured has furnished monthly statements to the Company, as compared with such average for the same months of the preceding year;

   (c) the amount determined under (a) above, increased or decreased by the percentage calculated under (b) above, shall be the agreed total amount of accounts receivable as of the last day of the fiscal month in which said loss occurs;

   (d) the amount determined under (c) above shall be increased or decreased in conformity with the normal fluctuations in the amount of accounts receivable during the fiscal month involved, due consideration being given to the experience of the business since the last day of the last fiscal month for which statement has been rendered.

   There shall be deducted from the total amount of accounts receivable, however established, the amount of such accounts evidenced by records not lost or damaged, or otherwise established or collected by the Insured, and an amount to allow for probable bad debts which would normally have been uncollectible by the Insured. On deferred payment accounts receivable, unearned interest and service charges shall be deducted.

7. **SETTLEMENT OF CLAIMS; ACTION AGAINST COMPANY:** All adjusted claims shall be paid or made good to the Insured within thirty days after presentation and acceptance of satisfactory proof of interest and loss at the office of the Company. No action shall lie against the Company unless, as a condition precedent thereto, there shall have been full compliance with all the terms of this Insuring Agreement nor at all unless commenced within two years after the discovery by the Insured of the occurrence which gives rise to the loss. If this limitation of time is shorter than that prescribed by any statute controlling the construction of this Insuring Agreement, the shortest permissible statutory limitation in time shall govern and shall supersede the time limitation herein stated.

8. **CHANGES:** Notice to any agent or knowledge possessed by any agent or by any other person shall not effect a waiver or change in any part of this Insuring Agreement, or estop the Company from asserting any right under the terms of this Insuring Agreement, nor shall the terms of this Insuring Agreement be waived or changed, except by endorsement issued to form a part of this Insuring Agreement.

INAPPLICABLE POLICY CONDITIONS

Paragraph 1A, 1F, 1G, 1H, 1I and 1N of General Policy Conditions do not apply to this Insuring Agreement

All other terms and conditions of the Policy not in conflict herewith remain unchanged.

Business Interruption

1. **SUBJECT OF INSURANCE AND PERILS INSURED:** This Insuring Agreement covers against loss resulting directly from necessary interruption of business as a direct result of all risk of physical loss or damage from any cause (except as hereinafter excluded) to the following property owned, leased, rented or under the control of the Insured:

   A. Data processing systems, computer systems or other electronic control equipment including component parts thereof;

   B. Active data processing media meaning all forms of converted data and/or program and/or instruction vehicles employed in the Insured's data processing or production operation except the following_____ _____

   which the Insured elects not to insure hereunder.

   This Insuring Agreement is extended to include actual loss as covered hereunder when as a direct result of a peril insured against the premises in which the property is located is so damaged as to prevent access to such property.

2. **MEASURE OF RECOVERY:** In the event such loss or damage results in either a total or partial suspension of business then this Company shall be liable:

   A. for the amount stated in the "Declarations" for each working day during the period of such total suspension of business; or

   B. in the event of partial suspension, for such proportion of the amount stated in the "Declarations" for each working day of total production which would have been obtained during the period of partial suspension had no damage occurred;

   commencing with the date of damage or destruction, and not limited by the expiration date of this Insuring Agreement, as would be required through the exercise of due diligence and dispatch to rebuild, repair or replace such described property as has been damaged or destroyed but in no event to exceed the amount of insurance provided.

3. **RESUMPTION OF OPERATIONS:** It is a condition of this insurance that if the Insured could reduce the loss resulting from the interruption of business.

   A. by complete or partial resumption of operation of the property herein described, whether damaged or not, or

   B. by making use of other property at the location(s) described herein or elsewhere, or

   C. by making use of stock at the location(s) described herein or elsewhere, such reduction shall be taken into account in arriving at the amount of loss hereunder.

4. **EXPENSE TO REDUCE LOSS:** This Insuring Agreement also covers such expenses as are necessarily incurred for the purpose of reducing any loss under this Insuring Agreement (except expense incurred to extinguish a fire), but in the absence of prior authorization by this Company or its adjuster, NOT EXCEEDING THE AMOUNT BY WHICH THE LOSS UNDER THIS POLICY IS THEREBY REDUCED.

5. **INTERRUPTION BY CIVIL AUTHORITY:** This Insuring Agreement is extended to include the actual loss sustained by the Insured, resulting directly from an interruption of business as covered hereunder, during the length of time, not exceeding 2 consecutive weeks, when, as a direct result of damage to or destruction of property adjacent to the premises herein described by the peril(s) insured against, access to such described premises is specifically prohibited by order of civil authority.

6. **EXCLUSIONS:** It is a condition of the insurance that the Company shall not be liable for Total or Partial suspension incurred as a result of:

   A. Any local or State ordinance or law regulating construction or repair of buildings;

   B. The suspension, lapse or cancellation of any lease, license, contract or order;

   C. Interference at premises by strikers or other persons with repairing or replacing the property damage or destroyed or with the resumption or continuation of the Insured's occupancy;

   D. Loss or destruction of accounts, bills, evidences of debt, valuable papers, records, abstracts, deeds, manuscripts or other documents except as they may be converted to data processing media form and then only in that form;

   E. Loss of or damage to property rented or leased to others while away from the premises of the Insured;

   F. Error in machine programming or instructions to machine;

   G. Inherent vice, wear, tear, gradual deterioration or depreciation;

   H. Any dishonest, fraudulent or criminal act by any Insured, a partner therein or an officer, director or trustee thereof, whether acting alone or in collusion with others;

   I. Damage due to mechanical failure, faulty construction, error in design unless fire or explosion ensues, and then only for loss, damage, or expense caused by such ensuing fire or explosion;

   J. Short circuit, blow-out, or other electrical disturbance, other than lightning, within electrical apparatus, unless fire or explosion ensues and then only for loss, damage or expense caused by such ensuing fire or explosion;

   K. Delay or loss of market;

   L. War risks or nuclear risks as excluded in the Policy to which this Insuring Agreement is attached.

(over)

245

7. **WORK DAY:** The words "work day", however modified, whenever used in this Insuring Agreement shall be held to cover a period of twenty-four hours and shall mean a day on which the operations of the Insured are usually performed.

8. **DEDUCTIBLE:** Each and every loss occurring hereunder shall be adjusted separately and from the amount of each such loss when so adjusted the amount indicated in the "Declarations" shall be deducted.

All other terms and conditions of the Policy not in conflict herewith remain unchanged.

ILLUSTRATION CREDITS

1.
Original drawing by Charles F. Hemphill, Jr. Originally appeared in "Planning a Security Program," *Security World*, October 1972. © Charles F. Hemphill, Jr. 1972.

2.
Fort Wayne (Ind.) *Journal-Gazette*

3.
Fresno Bee

4.
No specific source attributable.

5.
Diebold, Incorporated, Canton, O.

6.
Fort Wayne (Ind.) *Journal-Gazette*

7.
Photographs by Dr. Cliff W. Hemming, Jr.

8.
California State Highway Patrol

9.
California State Highway Patrol

10.
E. I. Du Pont de Nemours & Co. and Fenwal, Inc.

11.
E. I. Du Pont de Nemours & Co. and Fenwal, Inc.

12.
Lawrence (Kans.) *Journal World*

13.
Lawrence (Kans.) *Journal World*

14.
Alarm Lock Corporation, Los Angeles

15.
Upper, Simplex Lock Corporation, Brooklyn
Lower, Alarm Lock Corporation, Los Angeles

16.
Rusco Electronic Systems, Pasadena

17.
Eaton Yale and Towne, Inc., Charlotte, N.C.

18.
KMS Security Systems, Roseville, Mich.

19.
Mardix Security Systems, Mountain View, Calif.

20.
Original drawing by John M. Hemphill

21.
Original drawing by John M. Hemphill

22.
Original drawing by John M. Hemphill

23.
Original drawing by John M. Hemphill

24.
The Dow Chemical Company

25.
The Dow Chemical Company

26.
From W. D. Tiffany, "Are Computer Files Vulnerable to Magnets?" *The Office*, September 1972, p. 52. Reproduced by permission.

27.
The Dow Chemical Company

28.
Fresno Bee

29.
Lawrence (Kans.) *Journal World*

30.
KYBE Corporation, Waltham, Mass.

31.
Burlington Industrial Fabrics Company, New York

INDEX

This book has been set in 10 point Palatino leaded 3 points and 9 point Palatino leaded 2 points. Chapter numbers are set in 54 point Palatino; chapter titles are set in 12 point Palatino Semibold (lino). The size of the type page is 28 by 44½ picas.

.

Earl 2/21/02

DATE DUE